MOHAMMED JABBᴀ.

Islam
AND THE WEST

Throwing new light on one of the greatest
issues facing the world today

MOHAMMED JABBAR

Islam
AND THE WEST

Throwing new light on one of the greatest
issues facing the world today

MEREO
Cirencester

Mereo Books

1A The Wool Market Dyer Street Cirencester Gloucestershire GL7 2PR
An imprint of Memoirs Publishing www.mereobooks.com

Islam and the West: a rational perspective: 978-1-86151-298-7

First published in Great Britain in 2014
by Mereo Books, an imprint of Memoirs Publishing

Copyright ©2014

Mohammed Jabbar has asserted his right under the Copyright Designs and Patents
Act 1988 to be identified as the author of this work.

A CIP catalogue record for this book is available from the British Library.

This book is sold subject to the condition that it shall not by way of trade or otherwise be lent,
resold, hired out or otherwise circulated without the publisher's prior consent in any form of
binding or cover, other than that in which it is published and without a similar condition,
including this condition being imposed on the subsequent purchaser.

The address for Memoirs Publishing Group Limited can be found at
www.memoirspublishing.com

The Memoirs Publishing Group Ltd Reg. No. 7834348

The Memoirs Publishing Group supports both The Forest Stewardship Council® (FSC®) and
the PEFC® leading international forest-certification organisations. Our books carrying both the
FSC label and the PEFC® and are printed on FSC®-certified paper. FSC® is the only
forest-certification scheme supported by the leading environmental organisations including
Greenpeace. Our paper procurement policy can be found at
www.memoirspublishing.com/environment

Typeset in 11/15pt Bembo
by Wiltshire Associates Publisher Services Ltd. Printed and bound in Great Britain by
Printondemand-Worldwide, Peterborough PE2 6XD

This book is dedicated to the dissemination of rational thought and to the revolutionaries who have given their lives in the struggle against oppression.

Not to forget the memory of my dear parents, the late Mr Sheikh M. A. Jabbar and the late Mrs Jahanara K. Jabbar, to whom I owe so much.

"Not my god and not your god but our god,
for there is only one god, most gracious most merciful."

CONTENTS

Preface

Introduction

Chapter 1	The Qur'an – The Word of ALLAH (the Recital)	P. 1
Chapter 2	Selected Chapters (Surahs) of The Holy qur'an: Al-Mulk (Sovereignty), Al-Humaza (scandal-monger), Al-Ma'un (Charity), An-Nasr (Triumph), Al-Ikhlas (Unity), Al-Falaq (The Dawn), An-Nas (Mankind).	P. 14
Chapter 3	The Five Pillars (Arkans) of Islam and the Seven Articles of Faith	P. 25
Chapter 4	Muhammad – "the Seal of the Prophets"	P. 41
Chapter 5	Succession and the Seeds of War and Division	P. 64
Chapter 6	Contemporary Islam and the Rise of Militancy	P. 84
Chapter 7	One Ummah: Revival of the Islamic Caliphate	P. 124
Chapter 8	The End of Time – the Hour Glass Shatters	P. 149

Appendices:

1 Prophets mentioned in the Holy Qur'an

2 Recommended Further Reading and Useful Websites

Author's Profile

بِسْمِ اللَّهِ الرَّحْمَنِ الرَّحِيمِ

PREFACE

In the contemporary world Islam is taking centre stage, not least in its appeal as a global religion with followers throughout Europe and the United States, as well as in its traditional heartlands, but also in the backdrop of the tragedy of 9/11, the subsequent toppling of the theocratic Taliban regime in Afghanistan and the sequence of events leading up to the occupation of Iraq and its bloody aftermath. The forgotten war in Chechnya, the genocide in Bosnia and the contentious 'Peace Process' between Israel and the Palestinians, the United States-led 'War on Terror' and the detention in Guantanamo Bay of suspected Al-Qaeda operatives in conditions defying the Geneva Convention, the ongoing war in Afghanistan and the continued threat of so-called Islamic terrorists or jihadists are just some of the factors that have brought about a renewed focus on Islam, both by the younger generation of Muslims and by non-Muslims. We must not underestimate the inspiration behind the Arab Spring and its potential to change the political landscape in the Arab World, not least the profound implications for international politics, regional security and global economic infrastructure.

Extremism has no place in Islam. At the same time extreme right-wing propaganda against Islam in all its shades and forms must be challenged.

I have seriously endeavoured through this book to bring to the reader a rational approach to the study of Islam, bringing the fundamental features of Islam into focus, stressing factual analysis and rational deduction. Numerous materials have been extensively sourced, meticulously studied and critically evaluated. I take this opportunity to apologize for any errors. I sincerely desire that this work will provide a platform that will inspire readers, especially young Muslims and non-Muslims, to engage in further faith-based research of their own and hopefully find answers to questions that trouble those young inquisitive minds.

This book should also be useful to anyone who wishes to gain a first-hand, lucid and brief introduction to a faith of vast magnitude at different academic levels. Knowledge of Islam is not and should not be the exclusive domain of so-called 'Mullahs'. Rather every Muslim must make a conscientious effort to understand the core message of Islam so that they may not be led astray. The quotations from the Holy Qur'an and numerous Ahadith collections are not always exhaustive in relation to the subject matter being dealt with. Here I have exercised discretion in the selection of relevant verses. I strongly believe that this treatise on Islam will challenge many misconceptions of the Islamic Faith often drummed up by vested interests in achieving their political agenda.

This discourse also seeks to address the contentious issue of whether Islam or its so-called radical interpretation presents the most significant challenge to the worldwide predominance of Western democracy and capitalism since the end of the Cold War, as well as exploring the issues relating to the revival of an Islamic caliphate.

This book is the first of five anticipated publications, with the second book expected to be completed in the near future.

I would like to strongly reiterate that in the course of this work no deliberate attempt has been made to overtly criticise any individual dead or alive, nor to belittle, discredit or bring into disrepute any religion, belief or practice. Neither is this work intended to prejudice the reputation, interests or security of any country or nationality but rather to promote intellectual dialogue and a healthy exchange of ideas.

Sheikh Mohammed Jakir Ahmed Jabbar LL.B (Hons), ACILEx
June 2014/Shaban 1435 A.H.

بِسْمِ اللهِ الرَّحْمٰنِ الرَّحِيمِ

INTRODUCTION

From the appearance of *Homo sapiens* to the present day and beyond, the miracle of birth, the life we live and the certainty of death and their place in the cosmos have been, and will continue to be, the driving force behind faith. Faith in a supreme Deity above and beyond material comprehension provides order amid chaos. Man takes back a modicum of control through surrender to God via prayers, sacrifices, piety and charity – core characteristics emphasized by all major religions. Faith has played a pivotal role in sustaining humanity. All the major religions began their journey as rebellions against oppression, ignorance and indulgence. Essentially, faith has been Man's redemption from himself. Religion has only provided shape and form to his faith.

Islam is one of the success stories of the world's religions. From the deserts of an inconspicuous corner of Arabia a mere fourteen centuries ago re-emerged a monotheistic faith that now professes more than one and a half billion followers (nearly a quarter of mankind) spread across several continents. Islam, which means acceptance and surrender, commitment and submission to the one true God, is the dominant faith in the countries of the Middle East, North Africa, much of East Africa down to Kenya, Soviet Central Asia, Iran, Afghanistan eastwards to include the South Asian countries of Pakistan, Bangladesh and Maldives to Malaysia and

Indonesia. Although they are a minority in India, Muslims there number more than 177 million. And while the official Chinese figure puts the number of Muslims at 17 million, at least 23 million is closer to the truth. Of the three major monotheistic religions, Islam embraces and embodies the fastest-growing body of religious believers in the contemporary world and after Christianity is the world's second largest religion.

Unlike Christianity, which is divided between Eastern Orthodoxy, Catholicism and Protestantism, Islam is far from being a private religion of personal conscience and ethics. Rather it is a complete way of life, governing every aspect of human interaction laid down by ALLAH through His Messenger, Muhammad.

Islam belongs to the same family of religions as Judaism and Christianity. The Patriarch of the three is the Prophet Ibrahim (Abraham), a descendant of Nuh's (Noah's) son Shem as illustrated in Chapter 57, Al-Hadid, Verse 26 of the Holy Qur'an: *"And we sent Noah And Abraham, and established In their line Prophethood And Revelation."* The three monotheistic religions are rays from the same lamp and barring some (albeit fundamental) differences (discussed later) have strikingly common grounds. All emphasize the unseen, eternal, omnipotent Creator, the most compassionate and merciful imposing His structured will on earth. Yet the seeds of enmity and distrust between Islam and Christianity planted many centuries ago between 1095, marking the seeds of the first Christian Crusade at the behest of the Papacy; 'Dues vult' (God wills it), and the penultimate Crusade of 1248, the tolerance preached by the Prophets, Iesa (Jesus) and Muhammad has been manipulated for vested political interests.

The medieval Crusades achieved nothing substantial in terms

of real power and influence; in fact the second Christian Crusade ended in defeat ,while the third Crusade was inconclusive. What the Crusades did achieve was the savage death of tens of thousands, violation of married women and widows and the sacking of wealth. The battle cry was more driven or inspired by an irrational craving for land and power dictated by the political realities of the day than spiritual advancement or the appeasement of God. The so-called 'Holy War' was sustained by barbarism and aggression in the name of glorifying God in the perceived defence of Christendom against the expanding and encroaching Islamic Empire.

However, it must be emphasized that like different strands of thread interwoven to make a fine tapestry, the affinity and heritage of the monotheistic religions is clearly narrated in Chapter 2, Al Baqarah, Verse 136 of the Holy Qur'an where it states: *" Say (O Muslims): We believe in ALLAH and that which has been sent down to us and that which has been sent down to Ibrahim (Abraham), Isma'il (Ishmael), Ishaq (Isaac), Ya'qub (Jacob), and to Al-Asbat [the offspring of the twelve sons of Ya'qub (Jacob], and that which has been given to Musa (Moses) and Isa (Jesus), and that which has been given to the Prophets from their Lord. We make no distinction between any of them, and to Him we have submitted (in Islam)."*

With a common monotheistic lineage, Islam requires Muslims to believe in all the revealed books mentioned in the Holy Qur'an. They are the Tawrat (Torah) revealed to Prophet Musa (Moses); the Zabur (Psalms) revealed to Prophet Dawud (David); the Injil (the original Gospel) revealed to Prophet Isa (Jesus) and the Qur'an revealed to the final Prophet and Messenger Muhammad. The Qur'an also mentions the Suhuf–i-Ibrahim (Scrolls of Abraham). By no measure or form therefore, is Islam an advancement or continuation of Arab paganism. In fact, the theme underlying the core message of Islam is its unrestrained rebellion against paganism, idolatry and religious bigotry repeatedly expressed in verses of the Holy Qur'an.

It is only when preceding revelation(s) became corrupted following distortions in the Divine texts as mentioned in Chapter 3, Al-Imran, Verse 78 of the Holy Qur'an, where it states: *"And Lo! there is a party of them who distort the Scripture with their tongues, that ye may think that what they say is from the Scripture, when it is not from the Scripture. And they say: it is from ALLAH, when it is not from ALLAH; and they speak a lie concerning ALLAH knowingly,"* that a subsequent revelation followed with Islam being the last religion or revelation as illustrated in Chapter 5, Al-Ma'idah, verse 3 of the Holy Al-Quran, where ALLAH proclaims: *"This day I have perfected your religion for you, completed my favour upon you, and have chosen for you Islam as your religion."*

Nothing comes between man and ALLAH in Islam. There is no requirement for spiritual intermediaries. The concept of priesthood is alien to classical Islamic tradition but is now prevalent in many Muslim countries, inspired by Christian missionary influence of the last few centuries. There is no hierarchy of authority to clutter the Islamic Faith. There is nothing comparable to an organised Church. Any personal financial contribution in the way of Islam, though encouraged, is nevertheless entirely voluntary. Though there are religious scholars (Ulema) there is no equivalent to the archdeacons, bishops, archbishops or popes that can be found in the Christian Church. Surely, there is nothing further from the truth than to compare the institution of the Vatican to the Holy sites of Mecca or for that matter Medina. When leading the prayer in the Mosque the Imam is only the first among equals. Religious authority in Islam resides in the Holy Qur'an and according to Sunni Islam the Hadith as well, to which every Muslim has ready access. The Holy Qur'an is available in its unaltered Arabic version (the standardized text commencing from the reign of Caliph Uthman) though it has been subsequently translated into numerous languages. Of the six authoritative collections of Hadith, the most authentic Ahadith are widely received as the Sahih Al-Bukhari and Sahih Muslim.

Followers of the Islamic Faith possess a collective morality. Though the nation-states comprising the 'Muslim Ummah' (world-wide community of Islam) may at times be immersed in bitter geo-political rivalry amongst themselves, in Faith, nevertheless, the vast majority of Muslims across the Globe (irrespective of national identity) are passionately united in their observance of the Five Pillars of Islam, if not in anything else, particularly in their declaration of the Shahada (oneness of God and the prophethood of Muhammad), as well as in their vehement acceptance of the Divine truth of the Holy Qur'an. It is this passionate affirmation that underlines the strength and mysticism that characterizes the rationale behind the resurgence of Islam as a global phenomenon, especially in the face of perceived persecution of Muslims, particularly in Palestine, Iraq, Afghanistan and not too long ago in Chechnya, Bosnia and Lebanon.

Western societies and governments fail to understand this and therefore fail to comprehend the Muslim 'psyche'. Capitalising on this, radical groups stir themselves into expressions of extremism. This only emphasises the importance of understanding and advocating the correct interpretation of the Holy Qur'an and not its dissection to single verses or even phrases from verses that serve extremist agenda, deliberately distorting the true meaning of the Holy Qur'an. While some will argue that the majority of Qur'anic verses are stand-alone verses imparting a separate call to the Divine, the caveat is that such verses must not be read out of context. Instead the Qur'anic verses must be read and understood within the Spirit of the Divine Call and Guidance.

From an inconspicuous corner of the Arab peninsula, within two centuries of the Prophet Muhammad's death, the Islamic Empire under its successive caliphs spanned three continents from Spain to the gates of China, absorbing the then formidable Sassanid Empire and two-thirds of the Byzantine Empire, ranking the emerging Islamic Empire larger than the self-destroying Roman Empire. This is not to say that Islam advocates aggression or war for the sole purpose of sacking lands, power or wealth, or to forcibly convert unbelievers. In fact this is flatly prohibited in Chapter 2, Al-Baqarah, Verse 256, of the Holy Qur'an, where ALLAH says: *"Let there be no compulsion in religion: Truth stands out Clear from Error: whosoever Rejects Tagut (anything worshipped other than ALLAH) and believes in ALLAH hath grasped the most trustworthy Handhold that never breaks. And ALLAH heareth and knoweth all."*

There is however, a clear obligation of self-defence upon Muslims. This is expressed in Chapter 2, Al-Baqarah, Verses 190-193 of the Holy Qur'an: *"Fight in the cause of ALLAH Those who fight you But do not transgress limits; For ALLAH loveth not transgressors. And slay them Wherever ye catch them, And turn them out From where they have Turned you out; For persecution Is worse than slaughter; But fight them not At the Sacred Mosque, unless they (first) Fight you there; But if they fight you, Slay them. Such is the reward Of those who reject faith. But if they cease, ALLAH is Oft-Forgiving, Most Merciful. And fight them on Until there is no more persecution And the religion becomes ALLAH's. But if they cease, Let there be no hostility Except to those Who practice oppression.."*

Unfortunately, in reality the distinction between aggression and self-defence has often been blurred, giving rise to misconceptions about the Islamic duty of Jihad. While this will be analysed in some detail later, simply put, acts of 'terror' resulting in the death of innocent civilians clearly transgress limits. Muslims are required to provide a measured but effective response to persecution that must be appropriately directed. Consequently, innocent civilians can never be legitimate targets of war or jihad. In fact such a course of conduct is prohibited in Islam.

Regrettably, however, in recent military campaigns where Muslims have been on the receiving end, Muslim civilians and non-combatants have been legitimate game, often dismissed in military terminology as 'collateral damage'. To take some contemporary examples: The Soviet invasion and occupation of Afghanistan between December 1979 and February 1989 resulted in more than a million fatalities, with more than five million Afghans fleeing to Pakistan and Iran. It is reported that in the 1980s half of the world's refugees were Afghan nationals. It is also estimated that another two million Afghans were displaced within the country, while three million Afghans, mostly non-combatants, were maimed or wounded. In July 2006, Israeli military incursions into Lebanon, in what is referred to as the second Lebanon War, resulted in 1200 people being killed, mostly Lebanese citizens, with UNICEF estimating 30% of them to be children. The Israeli authorities have persistently denied such claims, while the Israeli-government appointed Winograd Commission found that Israeli defence forces did not target civilians and that evidence of war crimes was biased and without basis. On the contrary, Human Rights Watch and Amnesty International alleged the use of "indiscriminate air strikes" by Israel that resulted in civilian deaths.

The Bosnian War between April 1992 and December 1995 bears testimony to targeted ethnic cleansing of the civilian Muslim population of Bosnia and Herzegovina. With UN Security Council Resolution 713 enforcing an arms embargo in the former Yugoslavia, the Bosnian Muslim civilian population (Muslim Bosniaks) were effectively denied their inalienable right to defend themselves against the subsequent Bosnian Serb onslaught that was supported by the Serbian government of Slobodan Miloševic and the Yugoslav People's Army (JNA). The genocide of Muslim Bosniaks will forever be remembered by the Srebrenica massacre and the systematic and targeted rape of Muslim women and girls, particularly in Eastern Bosnia during the Foca massacres. Many Bosniak women and girls were gang-raped repeatedly by Bosnian Serb Forces and sold as sex slaves. Estimates of the numbers raped are above 20 thousand. This was the most potent way Serbs could assert superiority and victory over the Muslim Bosniaks. The Srebrenica Massacre is Europe's worst massacre since World War II, and witnessed the execution of 8000 unarmed men and boys, with the United Nations proving impotent to stop the Massacre.

As a consequence of the Second Gulf War, Iraqi civilians have suffered enormously, not only in terms of fatalities but also in terms of the many millions of Iraqi civilians who have lost their homes, rendering them refugees. The United States-led invasion of March 2003, ironically termed Operation Iraqi Freedom, resulted in the occupation of Iraq. More than 500,000 Iraqis died (Lancet Survey) and not less than a 100,000 according to the Iraqi Body Count (IBC) in order to prevent Saddam Hussein's regime from deploying weapons of mass destruction (WMD) against the West, when what actually transpired was regime change.

As to Iraq's 2003 potential to deploy WMDs against the Western coalition and their Middle Eastern regional allies, this assertion subsequently turned out to be a myth. In fact, following the invasion, the US-led Iraq Survey Group (ISG) concluded that Iraq had neither stockpiles nor an active nuclear, chemical or biological weapons programme at the time of the war. As to the Western leaders who advocated the case in favour of invasion, they have always insisted that they acted on the intelligence advice that was available to them at the time, believing what they did was right. Little consolation to the tens of thousands of innocent civilian families who have lost loved ones due to violent deaths.

Ironically, the former MI5 Chief, Eliza Manningham-Buller, stated when giving evidence to the Chilcot Inquiry in July 2010 that she had advised the Home Office that Iraq posed a "limited threat" to the United Kingdom prior to going to war with Iraq. The findings of the Chilcot Inquiry will no doubt make interesting reading. With regard to the plight of refugees, in 2008, the UNHCR reported an estimated 4.7 million Iraqi refugees. Of them around 2 million fled to neighbouring countries and beyond, while 2.7 million people were internally displaced.

While there will always be politicised debate of who can be considered combatants or victims of war crimes, sadly, nevertheless, the worst affected are invariably going to be women and children. As a consequence of these long-term military conflicts many

Muslim women and children have been displaced from their homes and forced to flee to neighbouring countries, often falling victim to sex trafficking and prostitution. Tragically enough, many children have also been rendered orphans and left traumatised, with little support from their governments.

Fundamental to the understanding of Islam, both from a religious and a political perspective, is the appreciation of Tauhid (Faith in the Unity/Oneness of ALLAH). It has three facets, namely Faith in the Oneness of the Lordship of ALLAH (Tauhid-ar-Rububiyyah), the Oneness of the worship of ALLAH (Tauhid-al-Uluhiyyah) and Oneness of the names and qualities of ALLAH (Tauhid-al-Asma was-Sifat).

The first facet declares the Sovereignty of ALLAH over all creation. In Chapter 2, Al-Baqarah, Verse 107 of the Holy Qur'an, it states: *"knowest thou not that it is ALLAH unto Whom belongeth the sovereignty of the Heavens and the earth; and ye have not, besides ALLAH, any friend or helper?"*

Another verse of the Holy Qur'an making a similar pronouncement is Chapter 5, Al-Ma'idah, Verse 120: *"Unto ALLAH belongeth the Sovereignty of the heavens and the earth and whatever is therein, and He is able to do all things."*

ALLAH is the sustainer of all that was, is and shall be and there is no intercessor with Him save with His permission. ALLAH has no beginning and no end. He is the eternal absolute, the one and only Creator. His structured will transcends the Universe – all that is seen and unseen.

The second facet requires that none has the right to be worshipped but ALLAH alone, and in Him alone do believing men seek refuge, shelter and protection. They neither worship nor seek sustenance from the angels, messengers, prophets, saints, idols or celestial bodies. This is narrated in Chapter 1, Al-Fatihah, Verse 5 of the Holy Qur'an. Needless to say all Muslims make this declaration every day in their daily prayers: *"Thee (alone) do we worship, and Thine aid (alone) we seek."*

And ALLAH mentions in Chapter 67, Al-Mulk, Verse 29 of the Holy Qur'an: *"Say: He is the Beneficent. In Him we believe and in Him we put our trust. And ye will soon know who it is that is in error manifest."*

Again in Chapter 40, Al-Ghafir, Verse 60 of the Holy Qur'an, ALLAH states: *"And your Lord hath said: Pray unto me and I will hear your prayer. Lo! those who scorn My service, they will enter hell, disgraced."*

While in Chapter 3, Al-Imran, Verse 160 of the Holy Qur'an it says: *"If ALLAH helps you, none can overcome you: and if He forsakes you, who is there after Him that can help you? And in ALLAH (alone) let believers put their trust."*

The third facet refers to Divine attributes being vested in ALLAH alone. This is narrated in Chapter 7, Al-A'raf, Verse 180, of the Holy Qur'an: *"ALLAH's are the fairest names. Invoke Him by them. And leave the company of those who blaspheme His names. They will be requited what they do."*

It is commonly accepted that the Holy Qur'an and Hadith refer to 99 names/attributes. Some of those attributes/names are mentioned in Chapter 59, Al-Hashr, Verse 23 of the Holy Qur'an: *"He is ALLAH, besides Whom there is no other god;- the Sovereign, the Holy, the Source of Peace (and Perfection), the Guardian of Faith, the Preserver of Safety, the Exalted in Might, the Irresistible, the Supreme: Glory to ALLAH! (High is He) above the partners they attribute to Him."*

Again in Chapter 59, Al-Hashr, Verse 24, the Holy Qur'an

states: *"He is ALLAH, the Creator, the Evolver, the Bestower of Forms. To Him belong the Most Beautiful Names: whatever is in the heavens and on earth, doth declare His Praises and Glory: and He is the Exalted in Might, the Wise."*

Widely accepted as representing one third of the Message contained in the Holy Qur'an, as recorded in Sahih al-Bukhari, the doctrine of Tauhid is exemplified in Chapter 112, Al-Ikhlas, Verses 1-4: *"Say: He is ALLAH, The One; ALLAH, the Eternal, Absolute; He begetteth not, Nor is He begotten; And there is none comparable unto Him."*

There must be conscious acceptance of Tauhid and complete adherence to it in our everyday lives. Belief without practice has no place in Islam.

Physical representations (images) of GOD are forbidden in Islam just as they are in the Ten Commandments and the book of Leviticus in the Old Testament. Worshipping pre-conceived images of God is not a mark of faith encouraged by either of the monotheist religious texts. Islam, however, goes a step further. Physical representations of the Prophet Muhammad in any form, including statues and pictures, are also forbidden. Though Muslims are often provoked into reacting angrily when the Prophet Muhammad is depicted with libellous connotations in different media streams, Muslims, it must be remembered, do not worship Muhammad.

It would be too simplistic to label the Holy Qur'an as merely a book. Muslims believe it is the last of the Divine Revelations. It is the principal source of Islamic Law/Shari'ah. It is the word of ALLAH, a recital of the dialogue between the Creator and Humanity through the Prophet Muhammad. From a human perspective the Holy Qur'an has been described as a miraculous achievement of sublime artistry. For a one-time shepherd, and later a trader who could neither read nor write to produce such magnificent artistry is inconceivable in the backdrop of seventh century pagan Arabia. This will be further explored in the next chapter.

The followers of the Islamic Faith are an inspired people. This is reflected in their history. A major achievement of classical Islamic civilization was the preservation, study and dissemination of Greek scientific tradition of late antiquity that later formed the basis of Western science and philosophy. It laid the foundation for the 'Age of Reason', igniting the flame of the European Renaissance. It must be remembered that Renaissance European civilization took shape in the shadow of powerful and already progressive Islamic empires, such as the Ottoman and Moghul empires. Further back, when much of medieval Europe was reeling under plague and religious bigotry, Islamic culture was flourishing, expressed in its architecture and academic pursuits in the sciences. The cities of Cordoba, Seville and Toledo bear testimony to these advances under the rule of the Moors in Al-Andalus (in present day Spain and Portugal).

While the Middle East is often considered to be the traditional heartland of Islam, by no means is it today representative of the Muslim Ummah. More than two thirds of all Muslims now reside not in the Middle East but in the Asia-Pacific region, North and sub-Saharan Africa, with a sizeable number living in Europe. There are around 500 million Muslims living in the Indian subcontinent alone, representing almost a third of the Muslim Ummah. As a country, Indonesia has the world's largest Muslim population of 204 million. Around 44 million Muslims now live in Europe, about 6 percent of Europe's population. Many of them have the right to vote. In the United Kingdom, Muslims represent around 4.6 percent of the population and are second or third generation migrants. There are more Muslims in Germany than there are in either Oman or Bahrain. Interestingly enough, Saudi Arabia (the birthplace of Islam) has around 25 million Muslims, which constitutes only 1.6 percent of the Muslim Ummah, yet commands one of the strongest Gross National Product per capita incomes in the Muslim Ummah alongside the United Arab Emirates and Kuwait. From a concerted study of demographic trends in the Muslim Ummah it is evident that Islam will embrace the largest number of global religious adherents by the middle of this century. The report by the Pew Forum on Religion & Public Life published in January 2011 predicts that there will be around 2.2 billion Muslims by 2030, representing 26.4 percent of the world's population of 8.3 billion.

More than three quarters of the Muslim Ummah are adherents of Sunni Islam and comprise developing countries. Many are heavily resigned to elected dynastic rule, such as Bangladesh and Pakistan, while a sizeable majority of those populations live in abject poverty. We are witnessing with both hope and apprehension the wave of protests in the Arab World (Bahrain and Syria amongst them) against dictatorships and a move in favour of political pluralism. Crucial for Western policy makers is what form of government these new representative democracies will produce, particularly against the backdrop of Arab perceptions of Western interference in the region both past and present. Subsequent democratic elections may well produce non-secular governments. What the Arab world may end up with is fundamentalism through the front door. The same can be said of North Africa in particular,

Tunisia, Libya and Egypt. In fact, during Mr Morsi's presidency, Cairo witnessed widespread protests against a draft constitution in November-December 2012 with protesters branding it as pro-Islamic/Shari'ah oriented. At the same time, these countries may end up with pro-Western puppet governments backed by Western corporate stakeholders. We will explore this area in more depth in chapter six.

The principal theological split between Islam and Judaism arises over which of the two sons the prophet Ibrahim (Abraham) was prepared to sacrifice at ALLAH's command to show his obedience. Followers of the Jewish faith believe that it was Ishaq (Isaac), the younger of the two sons. The Holy Qur'an directly contradicts this, rendering a different account. Ibrahim (Abraham) had only Isma'il (Ishmael) at the time of the proposed sacrifice and Ishaq (Isaac) was born subsequently as a bounty to Ibrahim (Abraham) for his obedience. This is narrated in Chapter 37, As-Saffat, Verses 101-113: *'So we gave him, Ibrahim tidings of a gentle son. And when (the son) was old enough to walk with him, Ibrahim said: 'O my dear son! I have seen in a dream that I must sacrifice thee. So look what thinkest thou?" He said: "O my father! Do that which thou art commanded. ALLAH willing, thou shall find me of the steadfast." So when they had both submitted to ALLAH, and he had laid him prostrate on his forehead (for sacrifice), We called out to him, "O, Ibrahim! "Thou hast already fulfilled the dream!" Lo! thus do we reward the good. Lo! that verily was a clear test. And we ransomed him with a momentous sacrifice. And we left for him among generations (To come) in later times: "Peace and salutations To Ibrahim!" Thus do we award the good. For he was one of our believing Servants. And we gave him tidings of the birth of Ishaq, a prophet of the righteous. And we blessed him and Ishaq. And of their seed* are some who do good, and some who plainly wrong themselves."

The Holy Qur'an makes it clear however, that ALLAH is the God of all creation with the Prophet Muhammad as His last messenger sent to all mankind, not limited to any race or region and includes the Arabs and Israelites. This is made clear in Chapter 7, Al-A'raf, Verse 158, where it states: *"Say (O Muhammad): O Mankind! Lo! I am sent unto you all, as the messenger of ALLAH, to whom belongeth the sovereignty of the heavens and the earth. There is no God but He: it is He that giveth both life and death. So believe in ALLAH and His Messenger, the prophet who can neither read nor write, who believeth in ALLAH and in His words and follow him that happily ye may be led aright."*

With Christianity the theological split essentially lies with the concept of Trinity, Islam brandishing it as a form of polytheism and denying outright the divinity of Isa (Jesus) as expressed in no uncertain terms in Chapter 112, Al-Ikhlas, Verses 1-4 of the Holy Qur'an where it states: *"Say: He is ALLAH, The One; ALLAH, the Eternal, Absolute; He begetteth not, Nor is He begotten; And there is none comparable unto Him."*

Again in Chapter 5, Al-Ma'idah, Verses 72-75, the Holy Qur'an says: *"Surely, they have disbelieved who say: ALLAH is the Messiah, son of Maryam (Mary)." But the Messiah (Isa himself) said: "O Children of Israel! Worship ALLAH, my Lord and your Lord." Verily, whosoever sets up partners (in worship) with ALLAH, then ALLAH has forbidden Paradise to him, and the Fire will be his abode. And for the Zalimun (polytheists and evildoers) there are no helpers. Surely, disbelievers are those who say: "ALLAH is the third of the three (in the Trinity)." But there is no God but the one God. And if they cease not from what they say, verily, a painful torment will befall on the disbelievers among them. Will they not* turn with repentance to ALLAH and ask His forgiveness? For ALLAH is Oft-Forgiving, Most Merciful. The Messiah (Isa), son of Maryam, was no more than a Messenger; many were the Messengers that passed away before him. His mother Maryam was a saintly woman. They both used to eat earthly food. See how We make the revelations clear to them; yet see how they are deluded away (from the truth)."

Furthermore, it is stated in Chapter 19, Maryam, Verses 88-93: "And they say: the Beneficent hath taken unto him a son. Assuredly ye utter a disastrous thing. Whereby almost the heavens are torn, and the earth is split asunder and the mountains fall in ruins. That ye ascribe unto the Beneficent a son. For it is not consonant With the majesty of the Beneficent that He should choose a son. There is none in the heavens and the earth but cometh unto the Beneficent as a slave."

The Holy Qur'an does however confirm the birth of Iesa (Jesus) of a Virgin – Maryam (Mary), but only as a sign unto mankind. This is clearly narrated in Chapter 19, Maryam, Verses 16-21: "Relate in the Book (The story of) Mary, when she withdrew from her family to a place in the East. She placed a screen (to screen herself) from them: Then We sent to her Our angel, and he appeared before her as a man in all respects. She said: "I seek refuge from thee to (ALLAH) Most Gracious: (come not near) if thou dost fear Allah." He said: "Nay, I am only a messenger from thy Lord (To announce) to thee the gift of a pure son." She said: "How shall I have a son, seeing that no man has touched me, And I am not unchaste?" He said: "So (it will be): Thy Lord saith, "That is Easy for Me: and (We Wish) to appoint him as a Sign unto men and a Mercy from Us': It is a matter (So) decreed."

The circumstances surrounding the birth of the prophet Iesa (Jesus) are no doubt an affirmation unto mankind of ALLAH's omnipotence, compassion, mercy, and sovereignty over all creation.

Another crucial issue on which Islam and Christianity differ theologically is the crucifixion. In the Islamic narrative, Iesa (Jesus) was not crucified on the cross. He was taken unto ALLAH. Chapter 4, An-Nisa, Verses 157–8 of the Holy Qur'an states: *"And because of their saying: We slew the Messiah Jesus son of Mary, ALLAH's messenger - they slew him not nor crucified, but it appeared so unto them; and Lo those who disagree concerning it are in doubt thereof; they have no knowledge thereof save pursuit of conjecture; they slew him not for certain. Nay, ALLAH raised him up unto Himself; and ALLAH is exalted in power, Wise."*

To suggest the separation of Islam from the State overlooks the inescapable convergence of religion and politics. Islam, like Judaism and Christianity, is inherently political. If we turn back the pages of history the three major monotheistic religions essentially began as rebellions against persecution perpetrated by the political establishment of the time (whether such tyranny was religious, social, and economic or a combination of the three). It culminated in the successful defiance and in some cases the uprooting of the existing political order. Briefly, with Judaism it was the defiance of the Jewish people against the slavery of Pharaoh that brought them out of Egypt and ultimately into 'Israel'. With Christianity it was defiance against the Roman Empire and the misguided practices carried out by the religious establishment in the Temple of God in Jerusalem. With Islam it was defiance against the oppression of the leaders of Mecca who thrived on the trade generated from idol worship that subsequently led to the victory of Mecca by Muslim forces, the destruction of the idols housed in the Ka'bah and the banishment of idol worship in Arabia and the rest of the Islamic Caliphate with Mecca becoming the centre-point/spiritual capital of Islam.

The three monotheist religions were conceived from wars, but only in response to persecution. The Book of Exodus narrates how Moses and Joshua had to fight many battles in their search for the 'Promised Land', including the battle against the Amalekites. Christianity only saw the light of day when Roman Emperor Constantine had a vision of a figure of the Cross prior to his battle with Maxentius, which he subsequently won and in return declared that all religions including Christianity would be tolerated throughout his empire. This laid the platform for the spread of Christianity in the West. The turning point for Islam was the (bloodless) conquest of Mecca by Muhammad. The triumph over Mecca was the springboard from which the message of Islam spread across Arabia and beyond. Prior to that however, the Muslims had to fight several battles perpetrated upon them, mostly by the rulers of Mecca.

Muslims believe the Ka'bah in Mecca is the spiritual beacon of the soul. It marks the site of the first altar dedicated to the worship of the one true God built by the Prophet Adam. Prophet Ibrahim (Abraham) later rebuilt the foundations of the Ka'bah with his son Isma'il (Ishmael) as stated in Chapter 2, Al-Baqarah, Verse 127 of the Holy Qur'an: *"And remember when Ibrahim (Abraham) and his son Isma'il (Ishmael) were raising the foundations of the House (With this prayer): "Our Lord! Accept (this service) from us: Verily you are the All-Hearing, the All-Knowing."*

The Ka'bah marks the Qibla (direction of salat/prayer) for Global Muslims. Most mosques will have a mihrab (wall niche) indicating the direction of salat. Though the Ka'bah is often termed the House of ALLAH, pilgrims do not worship the Ka'bah or the black stone encased in its eastern corner wall. From that perspective the Ka'bah is a brick structure. In Islam all worship is for ALLAH alone – the unseen one true God. The first qibla for the early Muslims was the Al-Aqsa Mosque in the Old City of Jerusalem. The change in direction of prayer followed a revelation the Prophet Muhammad received after His flight to Medina. This is illustrated in Chapter 2, Al-Baqarah, verse 150: *"And from wheresoever you start forth (for prayers), turn your face in the direction of the sacred mosque (at Mecca), and wheresoever you are, turn your faces towards it (when your pray) so that men may have no argument against you except those of them that are the wrongdoers, so fear them not, but fear Me! – And so that I may complete My Blessings on you and you may be guided."*

Islam, as a code of life, professes liberation from the evil indulgences that tempt the soul, not least the 'seven deadly sins'. Far from being a restraint on one's personal freedom, faith in Islam is an expression of one's spiritual liberation and intellectual enlightenment.

In the 7th Century, when women were treated as chattels with little or no rights guaranteed by the societies in which they lived, be it Europe, Africa, Asia, including the Arab peninsula, Islam gave women rights that had Divine sanction. For example, women were given rights of inheritance, the right to choose their husbands, the right to divorce, the right to learn and the right to carry on in business. The right most often misunderstood by some Feminist groups and the Western media is the right of women to command respect from their male counterparts through the concept of the 'veil'. This is narrated in Chapter 24, An-Nur, Verses 30-31 of the Holy Qur'an: *"Say to the believing men to lower their gaze and guard their modesty. That is purer for them. Lo! ALLAH is aware of what they do. And say to the believing women that they should lower their gaze, and* guard their modesty; that they should display of their adornment only that which is (ordinarily) apparent, that they should draw their veils over their bosoms, and not reveal their beauty except to their husbands, their fathers, their husbands' fathers, their sons, their husbands' sons, their brothers or their brothers' sons, or their sisters' sons, or their women, or their slaves, or male attendants who lack vigour, or children who know naught of women's nakedness. And they should not strike their feet so as to reveal what they hide of their adornment. And O ye Believers! Turn unto ALLAH together, in order that ye may be successful."

For many Muslim women the veil marks their religious and sometimes cultural identity, particularly those living in the West. It is a subtle political statement of their individuality.

Though polygamy is permitted in Islam, it requires that each wife be treated equally. Chapter 4, An–Nisa, Verse 3 states: "...Marry women of your choice, two or three or four; and if ye fear that ye cannot do justice (to so many) than one (only) or that which your right hands possess. Thus it is more likely that ye will not do injustice."

Debate surrounds the concept of equality. Some view it in materialistic terms, i.e. financial equality. Others enjoin the requirement of emotional equality, i.e. to treat each of the wives with equal emotional devotion. Too often do men take on further wives for the sole purpose of satisfying their sexual desires, often at the cost of emotional turmoil with the existing family. This is not the way of Islam, for polygamy in Islam is not a licence for debauchery.

Nikah (marriage) is a legal contract where the parties are free to agree upon its terms. This is particularly so when it comes to the Mehr (free gift) that is payable by the groom at the time of marriage, though there are provisions for all or part of the Mehr to be deferred. In which case, if the husband dies or the spouses get divorced before full payment, the Mehr debt becomes payable immediately. In Western matrimonial law it is very much akin to a pre-nuptial agreement. The Mehr provides the wife with financial security and independence, for it is hers to save or spend as she pleases. The Mehr becomes her exclusive property. In many countries though, it is the bride's father or guardian who establishes the marriage contract in her name. It should be emphasized here that the Mehr is not akin to a 'bridal-price' or dowry.

The practice of forced marriage is alien to Islam. In those Muslim societies where dowry is commonplace and where Muslim girls are encouraged to agree to arranged marriages, it is more of a cultural practice and has nothing to do with Islam. Furthermore, the nikah must not be viewed as a contract for the sale of goods (here the prospective wife) with the Mehr forming the consideration or price. As far as the treatment of the wife goes, the Prophet Muhammad reminded the Ummah in His Last Sermon that a wife should be treated fairly and that both husband and wife have corresponding rights over each other.

The Holy Qur'an forbids Muslims to marry idol worshippers until they worship the one true God, i.e., ALLAH alone. This is narrated in Chapter 2, Al-Baqarah, verse 221 where it states, *"And marry not the idolatresses till they believe;"*... *"And do not give your daughters in marriage to idolaters till they believe ..."* This is not to say that Muslims who have or are likely to marry idol worshippers should be subjected to violence or have their marriages annulled. Transgression of this sort is not the way of Islam. Then again, the marriage of Muslims to people of the Scriptures, i.e. Christians and Jews, is permitted. This is stated in Chapter 5, Al-Ma'idah, Verse 5 of the Holy qur'an where it states, *"This day are (all) good things made lawful for you."… "And (lawful in marriage are) chaste women who are believers and chaste women of those who received the Scripture before you when ye give them their marriage portions and live with them in honour, not in fornication, nor taking them as secret concubines. Whoso denieth the faith, his work is vain and he will be among the losers in the Hereafter."*

Divorce is frowned upon and is viewed only as an unavoidable recourse of last resort where all efforts at reconciliation have failed. Chapter 2, Al-Baqarah and Chapter 65, At-Talaq of the Holy Qur'an deals extensively with the issue of divorce. Though the husband may divorce his wife unilaterally by pronouncing talaq three times, the first two pronouncements must be followed by a waiting period to ascertain whether or not the wife is pregnant. If she is with child, reconciliation is preferred but if the divorce does, nevertheless, go ahead then the mother will have custody of a male child until he is the age of 7 or have custody until puberty in case of a female child. Financial allowances are to be made by the husband during the term of the pregnancy and for nursing the child, in which case care of the mother rests with the father. Under Shari'ah, the wife may also initiate a divorce to release herself from the contract of marriage where the marriage has broken down subject to a waiting period and attempts to effect reconciliation have failed. This form of divorce is referred to as faskh. The spouses may also divorce by mutual consent (khul) that takes the form of legal renunciation of the marriage contract.

Both men and women are accountable for their own actions before ALLAH. Islam applies equally to both genders in the spiritual context of the Hereafter and Judgement Day.

The derogatory image often portrayed by vested right-wing

elements against Islam in the context of gender equality lies not with the Faith but more with the different interpretations of the Divine Texts practised in different parts of the Muslim Ummah as the Ulema find it increasingly difficult to reconcile with modernity. Consequently, the applications of Shari'ah with regard to women's rights vary between Muslim Countries. However, as many developing Muslim countries do embrace modernity as an inevitable consequence of rural poverty, mass urban migration, birth control and the changing face of global consumerism this has meant an increasing emphasis by families to educate their female children. Consequently, as these countries prosper economically women are playing an increasing role in their countries socio-economic and political future.

We often find the term 'Islamic Shari'ah' being bandied about in different media publications. Let us briefly examine what Shari'ah refers to. It is the moral code of religious law in Islam. Literally Shari'ah means 'clear straight path'. Essentially, it is the enlightened path that leads to ALLAH. It encompasses rules for every aspect of spiritual, social and physical life. Among other things, it governs the rules relating to worship, ritual and conduct as well as legal matters. There are two primary sources of Shari'ah Law, the Holy Qur'an and then the numerous Ahadith, the latter embodying the Sunnah of the Prophet Muhammad. It is the Holy Qur'an that forms the main basis of Shari'ah Law. It states the principles, while the numerous Ahadith provide the details for their application. For instance, while the Holy Qur'an requires Muslims to establish salat (prayer) and pay zakat, it does not describe the complete details of how to do so. The numerous Ahadith provide those details. Both the Holy Qur'an and Ahadith may then be interpreted by the secondary sources of Shari'ah Law. They are Ijma (consensus) and Qiyas (human analogy or reasoning based on similar circumstances choosing the best solution). The secondary sources of Shari'ah only apply when a definitive answer cannot be found in the Holy Qur'an and then the Sunnah of the Prophet. Where a definitive answer is available in the Holy Qur'an, then neither the Ahadith/Sunnah nor the secondary sources can override this. But religious interpretation is never that black and white. Evidently there are shades of grey.

Fiqh is the science of Islamic jurisprudence. It refers to the 'understanding' of Islamic laws based on the Holy Qur'an and the Ahadith. There are multitudes of scholarly views within this science. However, within Sunni Islam four established madhahib (plural for schools of legal thought) have developed, with each madh'hab named after its founder. They are the Hanafi, named after Abu Hanifah Nu'man bin Thabit; the Maliki, named after Malik bin Anas, the Shafi'i, named after Muhammad bin Idris Al-Shafi'i, and the Hanbali, named after Ahmad bin Hanbal. Among the four schools of legal thought, the Hanafi School is the oldest and most diverse, being the official school of Islamic thought under the Ottoman and Moghul Empires. Rooted in history, the four schools have geographical delineations. Consequently, the Hanafi School is now predominant among the Sunnis of Central Asia, Afghanistan, Bangladesh, Pakistan, India, China, Iraq, Syria, Turkey, Albania, Bosnia, Kosovo, Macedonia in the Balkans and the Caucasus. Of the four schools, Hanafi is considered to be the most liberal, putting greater emphasis than the other three on ijma and qiyas. It would be safe to say that the different approaches of the four schools reflect their geopolitical history.

Within Sunni Islam all four schools of legal thought are respected as valid, promoting exchange of ideas and views between them. Nevertheless, stark differences appear in the way adherents of the four madhahib offer Salat (their daily prayers). This can often cause confusion among the young generation of Muslims living in Europe and America, where adherents of all the four schools practise their faith in the same smelting pot.

Halal (that which is permitted) and Haram (that which is prohibited) features strongly in the day-to-day lives of devout Muslims. Their everyday application can particularly be seen with respect to dietary rules. Muslims are allowed to eat meat, with the exception of pork, provided of course, the animal was killed while pronouncing the name of ALLAH by a clean and sharp knife severing the blood vessels. Muslims are not permitted to eat the meat of any carnivorous animal or dead carcass. There are however, exceptions, and that is when Muslims find themselves faced with extremities between starvation and eating haram or prohibited food. It could be agreed or reasoned that such instances would obviously include survivors of natural calamities and victims of war and conflict where halal food is in scarce supply. This is clearly stated in Chapter 2, Al-Baqarah, verses 172-173: *"O ye who believe! Eat of the good things that We have provided for you, and be grateful to ALLAH, if it is (indeed) He whom ye worship. He hath only forbidden you carrion, and blood, and the flesh of swine, and that on which any other name hath been invoked besides that of ALLAH. But he who is driven by necessity, neither craving nor transgressing, then it is no sin for him. Lo! ALLAH is Oft-Forgiving, Most Merciful."*

The consumption of alcohol is expressly forbidden and so is the sale of it by Muslims. This is evident from Sahih Al-Bukhari, Volume 5, Book 59, Hadith Number 590: *Narrated by Jabir bin*

Abdullah: That he heard ALLAH's Apostle saying in the year of the conquest (of Mecca) while he was in Mecca, "ALLAH and His Apostle have made the selling of wine (i.e. alcoholic drinks) unlawful."

Certainly, profiteering from the selling of alcohol falls squarely within the parameters of the above Hadith. There is nothing in the Holy Qur'an to contradict this analysis. In fact, Chapter 2, Al-Baqarah, verse 219 supports this: *"They question thee (Muhammad) concerning strong drink and game of chance. Say: In both is great sin. And some utility for men; but the sin of them is greater than their usefulness. And they ask thee what they ought to spend. Say: That which is superfluous. Thus ALLAH maketh plain to you (His) revelations that happily ye may reflect."*

The prohibition in the dealing of alcohol is therefore binding upon Muslims under Shari'ah. Interestingly, we do not find many Ulemas in the West being vocal in their respective communities discouraging the sale of alcohol by Muslim businessmen. This is particularly the case in the United Kingdom, where the catering trade forms the backbone of many businesses owned by Muslims. Many of these businesses contribute to the local mosques and madrassahs. Consequently, some Ulemas often cite the need of financial necessity. On the other hand, some Muslim scholars rebut this argument as farcical, exclaiming that a refusal to sell alcohol would only mean a reduction in profits. They also argue that these catering establishments can retain their non-Muslim customers by allowing them to bring their own wine rather than selling it to them. There is considerable divergence of opinion here.

It is regrettable that today the Muslim Ummah is in a state of decline, primarily because the Ummah has lost faith in itself (its own potential). This is essentially because the majority of Muslim states suffer from endemic corruption in all spheres of socio-economic life. We see a divergence from the teachings of the Holy Qur'an, underlined by an unrelenting pursuit of consumerism and selfish personal economic emancipation across the Ummah. Furthermore, Muslim States have lost faith in their ability to achieve economic emancipation attainable through the advancement of scientific learning based on an increased manufacturing platform. To add to its woes the Muslim Ummah has failed to effectively respond to modernity. Muslim states have either reacted irrationally to it or embraced it at the cost of their cultural and political identity as Muslims.

Other reasons for the decline include the lack of political pluralism and the overwhelming concentration and hoarding of economic wealth and political power in the hands of the ruling elite. Such economic wealth is often derived from the natural resources of respective countries (oil in particular), as is the situation in North Africa and the Middle East. It is hoped the Arab Spring will benefit the populations of those countries rather than amount to a change in the political 'Old Guard' only. Meanwhile, there has been an increasing trend of the ruling elite in some of those countries towards investing their oil-generated wealth outside their own countries for fear of the potential political turmoil that has now gripped the region. The Arab Spring has shown an increasing willingness of citizens to defy the autocratic rule of their national leaders in favour of democracy. Then again, the tragic acceptance of elected dynastic rule in the name of democracy is often marred by feuding party political violence, as is the situation in both Pakistan and Bangladesh, which also happen to be the second and third most populous Muslim majority states in the Muslim

Ummah after Indonesia, restricting the Ummah's capacity for unity and growth. This will be picked up again in Chapter Seven. Importantly, global Muslims must resort to the promotion and dissemination of ilm (rational knowledge of Islam) if they are to be successful.

CHAPTER ONE

The Holy Qur'an – The Word of ALLAH (The Recital)

"Read! In the Name of your Lord Who has createth, Createth Man from a clot. Read: and thy Lord is Most Bounteous, Who teacheth by the pen, Teacheth man that which he knew not." Chapter 96, Al-Alaq, Verses 1-5.

Both from a physical and psychological perspective, the experience of the first revelation for Muhammad was overwhelming and intense. It is beyond the comprehension of our ordinary day-to-day life experiences to truly fathom what Muhammad went through. It came upon Muhammad unsought, launching Him into a spiritual realm He could never have imagined. In the month of Ramadan, in the year 610 AD while immersed in one of His frequent solitary meditations in a cave known as Hira at the top of Jabal al-Nur (Mount of Light), near Mecca, the archangel Jibrail (Gabriel) came to Muhammad, ordering Him to recite. Muhammad replied he could not recite. Then when he was ordered a third time and overwhelmed in Jibrail's (Gabriel's) embrace, the Prophet Muhammad recited verses 1-5 of Chapter 96 of the Holy Qur'an as mentioned above. The Prophet would later recall when on the mountain side that wherever he looked there stood before Him on the horizon Jibrail (Gabriel) in the form of a man saying:"O Muhammad! Thou art the apostle of GOD and I am Jibrail (Gabriel)." Following what can only be described a tremendous experience, the Prophet hurriedly rushed to his home, trembling under a blanket in the comfort of his wife Khadija. She later consulted her cousin Waraqa ibn Nawfal, who was learned in the Scriptures (Torah and the Gospel). On hearing from Khadija the experience of Muhammad, Waraqa expressed he had no doubt that what Muhammad experienced had been Divine revelation and that surely He was the Prophet as foretold in the Scriptures. In Chapter 61, As-Saff, verse 6 of the Holy Qur'an it states: *"And (remember) when Isa (Jesus), son of Maryam (Mary), said: "O Children of Israel! I am the Messenger of ALLAH unto you, confirming the Taurat [(Torah) which came] before me, and giving glad tidings of a Messenger to come after me, whose name shall be Ahmed." But when he (Ahmed, i.e. Muhammad) came to them with clear Signs, they said: "This is plain magic."*

The first revelation marks the commencement of Muhammad's Prophetic Mission. So momentous was this event that it would change the course of the future of mankind. The rest of the Holy Qur'an would be revealed in stages, piecemeal, over the 23-year period of His Prophetic Mission. This is mentioned in Chapter 17, Al-Isra, Verse 106 of the Holy Qur'an: *"And (it is) a Qur'an which We have divided (into parts), in order that you might recite it to men at intervals. And We have revealed it by stages."*

The Holy Qur'an is an expression of ALLAH's Divinity to mankind. Being the Divine word of God, it is the spirit that lies within the meaning of ALLAH's speech that is eternal. ALLAH speaks to Mankind through the Holy Qur'an and it is therefore 'light and guidance'. Indeed, the Holy Qur'an imparts spiritual knowledge apparent only to those who possess resolute faith in and deep understanding of the tenets of Islam. The word Qur'an means 'to recite'. Parts of the Holy Qur'an are a recital of the dialogue between ALLAH and the Prophet Muhammad directed to all Humanity. The Holy Qur'an is a universal scripture addressed to all Mankind and not limited to any chosen people.

FORM AND STRUCTURE
OF THE HOLY QUR'AN

The Holy Qur'an is divided into 30 equal Divisions and has 114 Surahs (Chapters) of varying length. The longest Chapter, Al-Baqarah, consists of 286 ayats (verses), while the shortest Chapters, namely Al-Kawthar, Al-Asr and An-Nasr, consists of 3 verses each. The entire Holy Qur'an has 6236 verses. The Surahs have two principal categories. Those Chapters revealed to the Prophet Muhammad in Mecca both prior to and after his migration to Medina are referred to as Meccan, while those Chapters revealed to Him in Medina are referred to as Medinan. Of the 114 Chapters, 86 are classified as Meccan while 28 are classified as Medinan.

The Meccan Chapters deal mainly with the doctrine of Tauhid (Unity and Oneness of ALLAH), Risallah (Prophethood of Muhammad) and Akhirah (the final accountability of mankind in the presence of ALLAH). The Medinan Surahs, on the other hand, deal with the Faith's ritualistic and legal aspects such as Zakat, Sawm and the Hajj, as well as rules relating to social, economic and state policies, rules for declaring war and dealing with war captives, rules for accepting converts and divorce proceedings, as well as rules of punishment for various crimes. The Medinan Chapters also emphasise the unified message of the past prophets, condemn the hypocrites and draw upon the finality of the Divine Revelation with the Prophet Muhammad as the Last Prophet. The longer Medinan Chapters appear towards the front of the Holy Qur'an, while the shorter and in most cases earlier Meccan Chapters appear at the back. This arrangement can be traced back to the original Uthmanic Codex of 650 AD. Sunni Muslims, in particular, believe that the order and sequence of the Holy Qur'an was Divinely inspired.

It may be noted that the Holy Qur'an puts emphasis on the way it is to be recited, placing importance on patience and understanding. Chapter 73, Al-Muzzammil, Verses 4 states: *"And recite the Qur'an (aloud) in a slow, (pleasant tone and) style."*

THE COLLECTION AND COMPILATION OF THE HOLY QUR'AN

The collection and compilation of the Holy Qur'an relate to three distinct but overlapping (interconnected) periods of time. They are the time of the Prophet Muhammad, the time of the Rashidun Caliphs, Abu Bakr and Umar and finally the time period of Uthman. In which case, the standardised copy of the Holy Qur'an was completed and dispatched to different parts of the then Islamic Ummah in 650 AD merely 18 years after the Prophet's death. Of them, the Topkapi (Turkey) and Samarkand (Uzbekistan) codices are claimed to be the original copies sent out by the Rashidun Caliph Uthman.

It is universally accepted by Muslims that the Prophet Muhammad could neither read nor write with the Holy Qur'an referring to the Prophet as "al-nabiyy al-ummiy", which has been interpreted as the "unlettered Prophet". There is no historical evidence to suggest that the Prophet actually wrote parts of the Holy Qur'an. The Prophet Muhammad would proclaim the revelations as they came to Him to His Companions, who would in turn memorise them. Often scribes, on the Prophet's instructions, would record the revelations using whatever writing materials were at hand. Chief among the scribes was Zayd Bin Thabit. It would be worthwhile realising that during the time of the Prophet Muhammad oral transmission based on memory was the preferred norm of communication, given that writing materials were in short supply. A guarantee of accuracy and authenticity was usually accepted where the exact same text was known from memory to a number of people.

What was not available during the Prophet's lifetime was a single material collection encompassing all the revelations in one place. This was not possible given the continuity of revelation that went on up until the time of the Prophet Muhammad's death. Furthermore, the need for a single codex was not urgently felt or considered necessary, primarily because many of the Prophet's Companions were Hafiz, i.e. they had memorised vast portions of the revelations marking the tradition of hifz (entrusted to memory). More importantly, Prophet Muhammad was alive Himself. The Islamic community had the Prophet to refer to on matters of Faith. This last point is narrated in Chapter 16, An-Nahl, verse 44 of the Holy Qur'an: *"(We sent them) with Clear Signs and Scriptures. And we have sent down unto thee (also) the Message; That thou (Muhammad) mayest explain clearly to men what is sent for them, and that they may give thought."*

Perhaps if the Holy Qur'an had been recorded into a single

codex during the Prophet Muhammad's lifetime, the Shi'ite critique that verses were dropped in the Uthmanic Codex would not have arisen. It must be stressed that the principal diversion between Shi'ite and Sunni Islam is not solely based on religious doctrine but more on politics over issues of succession and leadership following the death of Muhammad.

Shortly after the death of the Prophet Muhammad, Abu Bakr (the first Rashidun Caliph) at the insistence of Umar (the second Rashidun Caliph) commenced the task of bringing together all the revelations, both written and oral, into one volume. Abu Bakr entrusted this task to Zayd Bin Tabit. Sunni Scholars believe that the principal reason behind the initiative to collect the Holy Qur'an was the death of numerous Qurra (those who could recite the Qur'an from memory) at the Battle of Yamama and the fear that large parts of the Holy Qur'an would be lost unless collected together, as many more Quranic reciters might die on other battlefields. This is narrated in Sahih Al-Bukhari, Volume 6, Book 61, Hadith Number 509. With an expanding Ummah founded on religious doctrine, it became all the more imperative to compile the Holy Qur'an to prevent inconsistencies in the Divine Text that could fracture the emerging Ummah on religious-political lines.

Heading the Committee of Compilers, Zayd Bin Tabit insisted on a number of conditions being satisfied before accepting any text as suitable for inclusion. They include the requirement that at least two reliable witnesses should testify that they had heard the same recital directly from the Prophet and the revelation was originally written down in His presence. Umar is known to have kept a complete copy of the revelations with his daughter Hafsah, who also happened to be one of the wives and then widow of the Prophet Muhammad.

It is understood that the collected revelations with Hafsah were not the official codex in terms of arrangement and dialect or public circulation. Rather it was during the rule of Uthman (the third Rashidun Caliph) that a major impetus was taken to compile a standardised copy. Again the task fell upon Zayd Bin Tabit. The traditional view is that along with Abdullah ibn Zubayr, Sa'd ibn al-As and Abdur Rahman bin al-Harith the official codex was prepared from the copy kept with Hafsah bint Umar but in the dialect of the Prophet's tribe of Quraysh. Copies of this official codex were then sent to different corners of the expanding Islamic Ummah. Any variant copies were ordered to be destroyed.

Given the increasingly turbulent rule of Uthman, one may ponder on the extent to which all different versions were destroyed. It must be remembered that the collection and compilation of the Holy Qur'an were taking place against the backdrop of the numerous wars the Rashidun Caliphs were engaged in, as well as the growing internal tensions between Ali and his predecessors to the Caliphate and their supporters. What the schism boils down to is a struggle for power between the Prophet's blood family and His families through marriage. The Islamic Ummah was expanding, rapidly bursting out of the confines of Mecca and Medina and engulfing the entire Arab Peninsula and beyond. This issue is dealt with later, in Chapter Five. Consequently, those who supported Ali's claim to the Caliphate over Abu Bakr, Umar and Uthman allege that the mus-haf (collected revelations) not only differed in arrangement to Ali's own collection but that the standardised copy produced by Ali's predecessors excluded all revelations with explicit references to the virtues of the Prophet's Family. However, there is no evidence to suggest that when Ali became the fourth and final Rashidun Caliph, he took steps to impose his collection of the Holy Qur'an (if any).

The Holy Qur'an itself makes representations that Divine Providence will secure its authenticity. This is narrated in Chapter 15, Al-Hijr, verse 9: *"Verily, We have sent down the Message and surely, We will guard it (from corruption)."*

In this context, the Holy Books of the Taurat (Torah) and the Injil (original Gospel) have been corrupted in the form of additions, subtractions and alternations in the original Text down the ages. The Uthmanic Codex has remained unaltered for the last fourteen hundred years.

MUHAMMAD AND REVELATION

While there are sensitivities and controversies surrounding Prophet Muhammad's role in relation to the revelations He received, nevertheless, the Holy Qur'an is a miracle attributed to Muhammad and the sign of His Prophethood. The nature and scope of this miracle is illustrated in Chapter 29, Al-'Ankabut verses 50-51 of the Holy Qur'an where it states: *"They say: "Why have no Signs been sent down to him by his Lord?" Say, "The Signs are indeed with ALLAH, and I am indeed a plain warner." Do they not think it is enough that We have sent down to you the Scripture that is recited to them? Verily in it there is mercy and a Reminder to those who believe."*

It goes without saying that the power of the written word is permanent and overcomes the constraints of time and place.

The Prophet Muhammad is understood to have said: *"Never once did I receive a revelation without thinking that my soul had been torn away from me."* The process of revelation was an exhausting experience for the Prophet, both physically and mentally. Occasionally a great heaviness would fall upon Him, His face covered with sweat and His body racked by convulsions. The revelations did not come easy to the Prophet.

There are two views, often considered competing, on the nature and modes of revelation. The traditional view that is taught in most madrassahs, particularly in the poorer developing countries, is that the Prophet Muhammad recited verbatim the verses as they were revealed to Him by the Angel Jibrail (Gabriel). The revelations would come to Him in a clear verbal form. The revelations were the words of ALLAH transmitted through the mouth of Muhammad. This is supported by the fact that there is a clear distinction between Muhammad's own speech and the linguistic narrative in the Holy Qur'an. The Qur'anic revelations are eloquent par excellence while it is inconceivable how the Prophet, who could neither read nor write, could produce such exquisite literary perfection. Its literary genre did not resemble any of the known poetic styles at the time or the rhythmic prose of Arabic literature. Furthermore, matters dealt with by the Holy Qur'an in terms of science are revolutionary by the standards of prevailing scientific knowledge in 7th century pagan Arabia. For instance, in Chapter 21, Al-Anbiya, verse 30, the Holy Qur'an states: "*Do not the disbelievers see that the heavens and the earth were a closed-up mass, then We opened them out? And We made from water every living thing. Will they not then believe?*" That it is ALLAH and not the Prophet Muhammad who speaks through the Holy Qur'an is evidenced by the way many of the revelations are addressed to Muhammad often by name, some prefixed by the word 'Say!' with ALLAH addressing the Prophet Muhammad in the first person singular and plural.

The non-traditional view is that like the other Rasuls, Muhammad had to struggle to make sense of the revelations, particularly so when they came upon Him not as dictated words but rather as visions or emotions. The Prophet Muhammad described them as sometimes coming unto Him like the reverberations of a bell, and that was the hardest upon Him, the reverberations abating when He was aware of their meaning. Both these views are enshrined, nevertheless, in Sahih Al-Bukhari, Volume 1, Book 1, Hadith Number 2: *"Narrated by Aisha: Al-Hartih bin Hisham asked ALLAH's Messenger, "O ALLAH's Messenger! How is the Divine Inspiration revealed to you?" ALLAH's Messenger replied, "Sometimes it is (revealed) like the ringing of a bell, this form of inspiration is the hardest of all and then this state passes off after I have grasped what is inspired. Sometimes the Angel comes in the form of a man and talks to me and I grasp whatever he says."*

It is worth noting that both views refer to a Divine Source of revelation. The revelations were therefore, not of the Prophet's own making, fabrication or forgery. This becomes clear from Chapter 52, At-Tur, verses 33-34 of the Holy Qur'an, where it states: *Or do they say: "He (Muhammad) has forged it (this Qur'an)?' Nay! they have no faith! Let them then produce a recitation like unto it (the Qur'an) if they speak the truth!"*

And again in Chapter 11, Hud, verse 13 of the Holy Qur'an it mentions: *Or they say: "He (Muhammad) forged it (the Qur'an)." Say: "Bring you then ten forged Surah like unto it, and call (to your aid) whomsoever you can, other than ALLAH, if you speak the truth!"*

While in Chapter 10, Yunus, verses 37-38 the Holy Qur'an states: *"And this Qur'an is not such as could ever be produced in despite of ALLAH; but it is a confirmation of (the Revelations) which went before it, and an exposition of that which is decreed for mankind – wherein there is no doubt – from the Lord of the Worlds." Or do they say: "He Muhammad has forged it?" Say: Bring then a Surah like unto it, and call upon whomsoever you can besides ALLAH, if you are truthful."*

In what can only be described as a compelling revelation,

the Holy Qur'an, Chapter 69, Al-Haqqah, verses 41-52 clearly states: *"It is not the word of a poet, little it is ye believe! Nor is it the word of a soothsayer (or a foreteller), little it is ye remember! This is the Revelation sent down from the Lord of the Worlds. And if he (Muhammad) had forged a false saying concerning Us (ALLAH), We surely would have seized him by his right hand, And then We certainly would have cut off the artery of his heart, And none of you could have withheld Us from (punishing) him. But verily, this (Qur'an) is a Reminder for the God-fearing. And verily we know that there are some among you that belie (this Qur'an). And indeed this Qur'an will be a source of bitter regret for the disbelievers. And verily, this Qur'an is an absolute Truth with assured certainty. So glorify the name of the Lord, the Most Almighty."*

That the Prophet Muhammad was Divinely inspired is further demonstrated in Chapter 42, Ash-Shura, verses 51-53 of the Holy Qur'an, which illustrate the modes of revelation: *"It is not granted to any human being that ALLAH should speak to him unless (it be) by inspiration, or from behind a veil, or that (He) sends a Messenger to reveal what He wills by His Leave. Verily, He is Most High, Most Wise. And thus We have sent to you (O Muhammad) Ruh (a revelation, and a mercy) of Our Command. You knew neither the Book nor the Faith? But we have made it (this Qur'an) a light, guiding with it whoever We will of Our servants. And verily, you (O Muhammad) are indeed guiding (mankind) to the Straight Path, the path of ALLAH, to whom belongs all that is in the heavens and all that is in the earth. Verily everything will return to ALLAH (for decision)."*

Divine inspiration is again evidenced from appreciating the processes of memorising, transmission and transcription of the Holy Qur'an as narrated in Chapter 75, Al-Qiyamah, verse 16-19: *"Move not your tongue concerning (the Qur'an, O Muhammad) to make haste therewith (memorisation of the revelation). It is for Us to gather it (in your heart) and to give you (O Muhammad) the ability to recite it (the Qur'an). And when We have recited it to you (O Muhammad through Jibrail), then follow its (the Qur'an's) recitation. Then it is for Us (ALLAH) to make it clear (to you).*

Further explanation of the above verses is provided in Sahih Al-Bukhari, Volume 1, Book 1, Hadith Number 5. While in Chapter 20, Ta Ha, verse 114 it states: *"Exalted be ALLAH, the one who is truly in control. And be not in haste (O Muhammad) with the Qur'an before its revelation is completed to you, and say, "My Lord! Cause me to grow in Knowledge."*

THE HOLY QUR'AN AS
A LIVING REVELATION

The Holy Qur'an occupies an unparalleled position to its reciters in comparison to other Divine Books. Madrassahs across the Muslim Ummah and beyond are churning out Hafize Qur'an (people who have committed to memory the entire Holy Qur'an) in their tens of thousands every year. Across several continents more than a billion and half practising Muslims recite verses of the Holy Qur'an in their compulsory daily prayers. The Holy Qur'an is therefore, a living revelation, not restricted to the confines of a book kept in the Mosques, Madrassahs or homes of Muslims. Rather, it is the heart of the Ummah that beats life into the souls of all Muslims every time it is recited. All attempts, therefore, to undermine the Holy Qur'an are futile. They amount to no more than bigoted steps adopted by ignorant people with the malicious intention of provoking a violent response by deliberately attacking the passionate sentiments of young Muslims. The 'International Judge the Qur'an Day' was a travesty beyond any rational comprehension.

It amounted to no more than bigoted theatrical rhetoric based on misinformation that had no meaningful substance. This followed the 'International Burn a Qur'an Day' sought to mark the ninth 9/11 anniversary. The 'accidental burning' of the Holy Qur'an at a US military base by US Forces stationed in Afghanistan, as reported in February 2012 by various media, is regrettable. Claims of the Holy Qur'an being desecrated by soldiers at Guantanamo Bay Prison as reported by different media streams in response to an inquiry that was sparked by a *Newsweek* magazine report (later retracted) that a Holy Qur'an was flushed down the toilet is equally deeply disturbing. An Inquiry led by the commander of the US detention center at Guantanamo Bay, Brigadier General Jay Hood, reported back in 2005, finding five instances of intentional and unintentional mishandling of the Holy Qur'an by US guards at Guantanamo. For the ignorant, the Holy Qur'an is alleged to be a book of war, with Islam posing a political and military threat to free people throughout the world, particularly in the United States. Taking this forward, it is worrying to hear of reports that United States military officers were being taught a course at a staff training college in North Virginia to prepare for a 'total war' against Islam and using 'Hiroshima-style tactics' on Mecca and Medina. We invite the sceptics to read the pages of the Divine Revelation setting aside their prejudices and try to understand its core message. It is understood that the Pentagon suspended the above-mentioned course in April 2012 following an -uproar.

CHAPTER TWO

Selected Surahs (Chapters) of the Holy Qur'an

Below is a brief explanation of some selected Surahs (Chapters) from the Holy Qur'an hoping that it will provide a platform for further academic research and study.

SURAH AL-MULK

In the name of ALLAH most Gracious most Merciful
Blessed is He in Whose hand is the sovereignty, and He is able to do all things- [1] Who hath created life and death that He may try you, which of you is best in conduct; and He is the mighty, the forgiving. [2] Who hath created the seven heavens in harmony. Thou will not see any fault in the Beneficent One's creation; look again: cannot thou see any rifts? [3] Then look again and again, thy sight will return unto thee weakened and made dim. [4] And verily We have adorned the lowest heaven with Lamps, and We have made them missiles to drive away the Devils for whom We have prepared the torment of the Blazing fire. [5] And for

14

those who defy their Lord We have prepared for them the chastisement of Hell; a hapless journeys end. [6] When they are thrown therein, they will hear its roaring in its breath as it blazes forth, [7] Almost bursting with rage every time a group is thrown therein, its keepers will ask them, "Did no one come to warn you?" [8] They will reply, "Yes indeed; a Warner did come to us, but we rejected him and said, 'ALLAH never sent down any revelation; Ye are in nothing but a grave error'!" [9] They will further say: "Had we but listened or used our sense, We should not now be among the dwellers of the Blazing Fire!' [10] So they acknowledge their sins; but far from mercy shall be dwellers of the Blazing Fire! [11] As to those who fear their Lord in secret, for them is forgiveness and a great reward. [12] And whether you keep your opinion secret or proclaim it, He certainly is the Knower of all that is in the hearts (of men). [13] Should He not know, - He that created? And He is the subtle, the Aware. [14] It is He Who hath made the earth subservient unto you, so walk in the paths thereof and eat of His providence. But unto Him will be the Resurrection (of the dead). [15] Have you taken security from Him Who is in the Heaven that He will not cause the earth to swallow you when it is convulsed (as in an earthquake)? [16] Or have you taken security from Him Who is in the Heaven that He will not send against you a hurricane? But you shall know the manner of My warning? [17] And verily those before them rejected (My warning); then (see) the manner of My warning (with them)! [18] Have they not seen the birds above them spreading out their wings and folding them in? None upholds them save the Most Gracious; Truly He watches over all things. [19] Or who is He that can help you as an army instead of the Most Merciful? The disbelievers are in nothing but delusion. [20] Or who is He that will provide you with sustenance if He should withhold His providence? Nay, but they obstinately persist in insolent impiety and flight (from the Truth). [21] Is he who walks headlong, with his face grovelling, better guided, - or he who walks upright on a straight path? [22] Say (unto them O Muhammad): "It is He who has created you and assigned unto you faculties of hearing, sight and understanding: Small thanks it is you give! [23] Say: "He it is who multiplied you through the earth, and unto Whom you will be gathered together." [24] They ask: When will this promise (be fulfilled), if ye are telling the truth? [25] Say: "As to the knowledge of the time, it is with ALLAH alone; and I am but a plain warner." [26] But when they see it close at hand, the faces of those who disbelieve will be grieved, and it will be said (to them): " This is (the promise fulfilled), for which you were calling for!" [27] Say (O Muhammad): If ALLAH were to destroy me (Muhammad), and those with me, or if He bestows His mercy on us, still, who will protect the disbelievers from a painful doom? [28] Say: "He is the Most Gracious. In Him we believe and in Him we put our trust: and you will soon know which (of us) it is in manifest error." [29] Say: "Have ye thought: if all your water were to disappear into the earth who then could bring you gushing water?" [30]

This Surah appears as the 67th in the Holy Qur'an and is widely accepted as being revealed in Mecca.

Among other things, the Surah expresses ALLAH's sovereignty and dominion over all creation. Unto ALLAH alone belongs the sovereignty of the Heavens and the earth and He is able to do all things. His power is infinite. He has created life and death to test Man's faith through his actions, yet ALLAH is forgiving to those who refrain from evil and seeks His forgiveness.

Having created the seven Heavens in perfect harmony, ALLAH challenges us to probe the Universe. As modern science continues its study of the Heavens, patterns and themes are emerging which fascinate and challenge our intellects. From the regular orbits of the planets to the creation of new stars and their violent destruction; from the expanding Universe to quantum mechanics, principles of gravity and the fact that everything is in relative motion, some sense of Divine instruction is clearly apparent. Being limitless, ALLAH is not confined to the parameters of our known Universe. He has no beginning and therefore no end. This is clearly stated in Chapter 114, Al-Ikhlas, verse 2, *"ALLAH, the Eternal, Absolute."* The Big Bang or as some call it the 'moment of creation' did not create ALLAH. ALLAH falls beyond the realms of our understanding of our known Universe. ALLAH is metaphorically described in Chapter 24, An-Nur, Verse 35 as *"Light upon Light!"* that which cannot be measured – both glorious and illimitable. Our understanding of ALLAH and His creation is limited to our human perceptions as stated in Chapter 6, Al-Anam, verse 103, *"No vision can take Him in, but He takes in all vision. He is the All Subtle, the All Aware."*

Those who disbelieve and defy ALLAH are warned of the dire consequences of hellfire. When in Hell, repentance will be of little consequence to them. To bring Man to the path of ALLAH, He has sent to humanity countless Prophets to deliver His message of forgiveness and retribution, with Muhammad being the last Prophet. There is promise of forgiveness and paradise for those who have faith in ALLAH, whether or not they publicly profess such faith or keep it secret in their hearts. ALLAH surely knows what lies in the hearts and minds of men. Muslims in the face of persecution must therefore hold strongly to their faith. Such conviction ensures success.

Through this Surah we are told that ALLAH has made the earth subservient to mankind so that we may cultivate it to grow crops from which we can derive our sustenance to survive. The Surah also prompts us to question our ignorance of religion by asking who could save us from natural calamities such as the convulsions of an earthquake, the winds of a hurricane or the failure of food crops. Recent manifestations of such natural disasters include the Haiti Earthquake in January 2010, the Boxing Day Tsunami of 2004 in Southeast Asia following a massive undersea earthquake, Hurricanes Katrina and Isaac, which hit the US in August 2005 and August 2012 respectively; the severe drought in East Africa in the summer of 2011 and most recently Superstorm Sandy, which hit the eastern US coast in October 2012. Like the Meccans, we too are warned of dire consequences for our avoidance of the Truth, like those civilisations before us.

Finally, ALLAH prompts the Prophet to say that ALLAH has brought Mankind into being, giving us the senses of sight and hearing as well as understanding; that it is ALLAH who has scattered humans across the Globe, only to be gathered on Judgement Day. Those who disbelieve will be horrified when the 'End of Days' befalls them. Then they will understand who truly is in error.

SURAH AL-HUMAZA

In the name of ALLAH most Gracious most Merciful
Woe to every scandal-monger and backbiter, [1] Who pileth up wealth
(of this world) And arranged it, [2] Thinketh that his wealth will make
him last forever! [3] No, but He will be sure to be flung to the
Consuming One, [4] And what will explain to thee what the
Consuming One is? [5] (It is) the fire of ALLAH, kindled, [6] Which
leapeth up over the hearts (of men): [7] It shall be made into a vault
over them, [8] In columns outstretched. [9]

Revealed in Mecca, this appears as the 104th Surah in the

Holy Qur'an. In essence, it condemns in no uncertain terms backbiting, greed and the selfish hoarding of wealth. As advocates of peace, Muslims are prohibited from indulging in mischief-making through spreading rumours resulting in scandal, or making innuendos, taunts or insults against others. Taking this further, idle gossip about others which unfortunately many in our society relish in practising should not be a character trait of believing Muslims and should be shunned. It is against the spirit of this Surah to seek to belittle others. Sadly, there are those in our community who, envious of the success of their fellow Muslims, will go to great lengths to dig up dirt in an attempt to cause them hurt and anguish without trying to better their own station in life. Muslims must live and thrive as one homogenous body.

We must be in a state of readiness to help and support members of our society, particularly the less fortunate and vulnerable. The accumulation of wealth for one's own benefit and making provisions for one's own family beyond their reasonable requirements is frowned upon in Islam. Muslims are required to desire for others what they desire for themselves. Living in palatial mansions when making no contribution to the uplift of fellow Muslims who live in shanties in close proximity is not the way of Islam. Very often do we come across wealthy families who indulge in extravagance and splendour and seem obsessed with a desperate pursuit of wealth, yet fail to provide support to their Muslim brethren, who struggle to make ends meet with their children going hungry, unclothed and without access to proper education. And yet ironically, these affluent families portray themselves as devout Muslims. In this Surah, ALLAH warns of dire consequences, narrating a harrowing description of fire as punishment against such selfish indulgences.

Being mortal, we must remember that the wealth we accumulate will stay behind us after our death. What we take with us to the Hereafter is our good deeds and Faith and nothing else. Rather, we will be made to account for the wealth we so much strive to amass.

SURAH AL-MA'UN

In the name of ALLAH most Gracious most Merciful
Have you observed him who belies religion? [1] It is he who repulses the orphan, [2] And encourages not the feeding of the needy. [3] So woe to the worshippers [4] Who are heedless of their prayer; [5] Those who want to be seen, [6] But refuse small kindness (even neighbourly needs). [7]

Widely accepted as revealed in Mecca, this appears as the 107th Surah in the Holy Qur'an. It reminds worshippers of the true meaning of prayer and Faith. The Surah points out that we must be sincere in providing charity and showing kindness towards the needy, destitute and orphans in society. It is not in keeping with the spirit of being a Muslim to shun an orphan, refuse to provide charity or encourage others not to be charitable. Those who are better off in society must remember that their wealth and social standing comes from ALLAH alone. In Chapter 6, Al-Anam, verse 165 we are told that we have been made inheritors of the earth, while some have been made more prosperous than others. There is no doubt that we will be tried with what we have been given, be it power or wealth. Transgressions will be met with by punishment. Yet ALLAH is often forgiving and most merciful. The wealthy and powerful therefore, have a corresponding duty and obligation towards the poorer sections of society.

The Surah reminds us that true worship does not take the form of merely offering prayers at the Mosque for the purpose of being seen to do so. Offering prayers without a clear conscience while constantly conniving and scheming to bring harm to others cannot be an expression of true Faith. Acts of charity are meaningless if we fail in our everyday duty to express kindness to our family, friends and neighbours.

SURAH AN-NASR

In the name of ALLAH most Gracious most Merciful
When ALLAH's succor and the triumph cometh; [1] And thou seest
mankind entering the religion of ALLAH in troops; [2] Then hymn
the praises of thy Lord, and seek forgiveness of Him. Lo He is ever ready
to show mercy. [3]

In order of revelation, this is the last full Surah revealed to the Prophet Muhammad only a few months prior to His death. Revealed in Mecca, Surah An-Nasr is the 110th Surah in the Holy Qur'an.

ALLAH proclaims through this Surah that He gave succour to the first Muslims throughout their many trials and tribulations that culminated in certain victory with the conquest of Mecca following which all the Tribes in Arabia eventually came within the fold of Islam.

From this Surah, Muslims today can draw strength and inspiration from the fact that despite being persecuted, whether it is in the form of external aggression by a foreign power or internal suppression lashed out by a ruthless despot, they should remain steadfast in their Faith and strive against such persecution in which case, victory will eventually be theirs. But when such victory is attained, Muslims must submit to their Lord in His praise and seek His forgiveness. For ALLAH is always ready to show mercy.

SURAH AL-IKHLAS

In the name of ALLAH most Gracious most Merciful
Say: He is ALLAH, the One; [1] ALLAH, the Eternal, Absolute; [2]
He begetteth not, nor is He begotten; [3] And there is none like unto
Him. [4]

Revealed in Mecca, it is the 112th Surah in the Holy Qur'an. Although only 4 ayats (verses) long it is a potent declaration of the doctrine of Tauhid (Faith in the Unity/Oneness of ALLAH). In a nutshell Surah Al-Ikhlas represents the very essence of the Holy Qur'an. It proclaims an absolute departure from idol worship practiced by Meccans of the time. Islam emerged essentially as a rebellion against paganism, idolatry and religious bigotry. ALLAH has no ancestry, for He has no beginning and no end. He is both Ahad and Samad, i.e. 'one and absolute'. This theme is further advocated by the Surah in its rejection of the Christian theological belief of Trinity. It declares that there is none comparable to ALLAH. All worship is for ALLAH alone, the unseen one true God. In ALLAH alone do believing men seek refuge, shelter and protection. Everyday across the Globe, Muslims confirm their Faith in the doctrine of Tauhid making this declaration in their daily prayers. There must be conscious acceptance of Tauhid and complete adherence to it in our everyday lives. Belief without practice has no place in Islam.

The indivisibility of ALLAH inevitably leads to the concept of the unity of the Muslim Ummah in its worship of ALLAH. It would serve Muslims well to do away with their geo-political religious factions that have done nothing but to weaken the

Muslim Ummah. To be strong, Global Muslims must be united in their worship of ALLAH Almighty, most Gracious most Merciful and identifiable as one homogenous religious body.

SURAH AL-FALAQ

In the name of ALLAH most Gracious most Merciful
Say I seek refuge with the Lord of the Daybreak, [1] From the evil of that which He created, [2] From the evil of the Darkness as it overspreads, [3] And from the evil of the malignant witchcraft, [4] And from the evil of the envier when he envies. [5]

Appearing as the 113th Surah in the Holy Qur'an it was revealed in Mecca and along with Surah An-Nas is an invocation against evil. The faithful seek protection from ALLAH, the ultimate source of Truth, whose light pervades the darkness of Man's ignorance allowing him to overcome evil. Daybreak and Darkness are dealt with metaphorically here. It is akin to the Dawn when night fades away ushering in daylight. Through this Surah the faithful seek refuge from their Lord against evil in its various manifestations, particularly from superstitious beliefs, the practice of witchcraft and from the scornful eye of the envious.

SURAH AN-NAS

In the name of ALLAH most Gracious most Merciful
Say I seek refuge with the Lord of Mankind, [1] The King of Mankind, [2] The God of Mankind, - [3] From the mischief of the Whisperer, who withdraws (after his whisper), [4] Who whispers into the hearts of Mankind, - [5] Among the Jinn and of Mankind. [6]

This Surah appears as the last in the Holy Qur'an and is believed to have been revealed in Mecca. Surah Al-Ikhlas, Surah

Al-Falaq and Surah An-Nas are collectively referred to as the 'three Quls'. The faithful invoke this last Surah in their daily prayers seeking refuge with ALLAH from Satan and his minions who seek to tempt Man and the Jinn to the path of sin. It is only through the practice of one's faith that Mankind can overcome the evil whispers/temptations of Satan. To this effect, the Prophet Muhammad in His last Sermon warned His Ummah to beware of Satan in matters relating to their daily life, as he is desperate to divert the faithful from the worship of ALLAH. Mankind's relationship with ALLAH is referred to in this Surah. In essence ALLAH is declared as the Lord and sustainer of the Human Race, thereby Mankind's Lord and King. No earthly King or ruler can provide Mankind with protection from the tribulations of the Hereafter, for all earthly rulers will themselves face Judgment Day. It is to ALLAH alone therefore, that Humanity must seek protection. Time and again in the Holy Qur'an it is mentioned that the sovereignty of the Heavens and the Earth belong to ALLAH alone who is able to do all things. He is the Rabb of everything as described in Chapter 6, Al-Anam, verse 164 of the Holy Qur'an where it states, "*Say, "Should I seek another other than ALLAH as a Lord while He is the Lord of all things? And every soul earns not [blame] except against itself, and no bearer of burdens will bear the burden of another. Then to your Lord is your return, and He will inform you concerning that over which you used to differ."*

CHAPTER THREE

The Five Pillars of Islam and the Seven Articles of Faith

The conception that there are five basic principles of the Islamic Faith was first conveyed in the Sahih Hadith Collections by Al-Bukhari.

Narrated by Ibn Umar: *"ALLAH's Messenger said, "Islam is based upon (the following) five (principles): They are the declaration of faith (Shahada) to testify that none has the right to be worshipped but ALLAH and Muhammad is the Messenger of ALLAH; offering of the (compulsory) prayer (Salat) dutifully and perfectly; paying wealth tax (Zakat); performing the pilgrimage (Hajj), and fasting during the month of Ramadan (Sawm).* (Sahih Al-Bukhari, Volume 1, Book 2, Hadith Number 7).

These had come to be called the Five Pillars (Arkans) of Islam by the tenth century AD.

SHAHADA

"La ilaha illal lahu muhammadur rasulul lah"
"There is no God but ALLAH, Muhammad is the messenger of ALLAH"

The Shahada, otherwise referred to as the Declaration of Faith, has two aspects to it but one core theme. The first aspect requires Muslims to confirm their faith in the Unity and Oneness of ALLAH (Tauhid) (which has been discussed at some length in the introduction). It declares the Monotheist doctrine of One God. Taking it from the Arabic: La means no; ilaha meaning God; illa meaning but; Lah meaning ALLAH. Importantly, the very basis of the Faith of Islam is expressed with a negative in defiance of Shirk (associating partners to ALLAH). All the Messengers of ALLAH have conveyed the message of Tauhid. The Holy Qur'an states this in Chapter 21, Al-Anbiya, Verse 25: *"And We did not send any Messenger before you (O Muhammad) without revealing to him: None has the right to be worshiped but I ALLAH, so worship Me (alone and none else)."*

Shirk is unforgivable sin. This is narrated in Chapter 4, An-Nisa, Verse 48 of the Holy Qur'an: *"Verily, ALLAH forgives not that partners should be set up with Him (in worship), anything less than that He forgives to whoever He will, but whoever sets up partners with ALLAH in worship, he has indeed invented a tremendous sin."*

The second aspect relates to Rishalah and confirms Muhammad's prophetic mission as the Messenger of ALLAH to whom was revealed the Last of the Divine Revelations in the form of the Holy Qur'an. The Prophet Muhammad was not sent to any particular nation or community but to all Mankind and for all time. In Chapter 34, Sabah, Verse 28 of the Holy Qur'an it states: *"And We have not sent you (O Muhammad) except as a giver of glad tidings and a warner to all mankind, but most men know not."*

The Prophet Muhammad is proclaimed by ALLAH as "Khatam-an-Nabiyyin" (the last of the chain of the true prophets). With Him, Prophethood came to an end. No other Prophet will come after Him. This is narrated in the Holy Qur'an in Chapter 33, Al-Ahzab, Verse 40: *"Muhammad is not the father of any one of you men; but he is the Messenger of ALLAH and the last (end) of the prophets. And ALLAH is Ever All-Aware of everything."*

One simple sentence, yet the Shahada stirs the soul of every believing Muslim. So tremendous is its effect when truly understood and appreciated that the early Muslims accepted martyrdom in face of persecution from the rulers of Mecca yet still would not renounce the Shahada. Pronunciation of the Shahada in Arabic with intent (with knowledge of its meaning), before two qualified witnesses, is all that is formally required to become a Muslim. Everyday during the Adhan (Call to Prayer), the Shahada rings out across the Muslim Ummah to which Muslims respond by offering their Salat thereby reaffirming their Declaration of the Faith. The central theme of the Shahada is therefore Unity of Faith in the religion of Islam.

SALAT

Central to the faith of Islam is the Salat, ie the observance of the compulsory five daily prayers with due care and attention. It is the second pillar of Islam. There is no necessity to take the assistance of spiritual intermediaries to offer the Salat. It can be offered alone in the confines of the home. All religions, monotheist or not, have a pattern of ritual prayer. In Islam it takes the form of Salat.

Having said this, the prime importance of Salat is that it brings the community together when offered in congregation (Salat al-Jama'ah), be it at the local Mosque or other religious meeting/gathering place. When offering Salat; irrespective of race, class or wealth, all stand shoulder to shoulder, united in their worship of ALLAH. The Imam (one who leads the congregational prayers at the Mosque) is only the first among equals. Prayers held in congregation provide unity and strength to Muslims. The daily prayers are preceded by the Adhan (Call to Prayer). Facing towards Mecca, the Muazzin (nominated person in the Mosque who makes the call to prayer) calls out to the locality that it is time to offer Salat at the Mosque. In Muslim majority countries 5 times a day the call for Salat (Adhan) rings out across the cities, towns and villages inviting Muslims to offer their prayers. The structure of the Adhan is in the following chronological order: "ALLAH is the Greatest" (4 times); " I bear true witness that there is no God but ALLAH (2 times); "I bear true witness that Muhammad is the Messenger of ALLAH" (2 times); "Come for Prayer" (2 times); "Come for Salvation" (2 times); "ALLAH is the Greatest" (2 times); "There is no God but ALLAH (1 time). During the early morning/Fajr prayers, "Prayer is better than sleep" is narrated twice before "ALLAH is the Greatest" towards the end of the Adhan. The five daily prayers have prescribed times that should be adhered to. To this effect the Holy Qur'an states in Chapter 4, An-Nisa, Verse 103: *"After performing the ritual prayer, continue to remember ALLAH, standing, sitting and reclining. And when ye are in safety, observe proper prayer. Prayer is obligatory for the believers at fixed hours."*

The names and times of the five daily prayers are as follows. The first is the Fajr (early morning) prayers, which commences after the break of dawn and ends before sunrise. It is made up of 2 raka'ats pre-farz sunnat and 2 raka'ats farz prayers. Then comes the Zuhr (early afternoon) prayers. This prayer must be offered after mid-day until afternoon. This Salat is made up of 4 raka'ats pre-farz sunnat, 4 raka'ats farz, 2 raka'at post-farz sunnat and 2 raka'at nafl prayers. Following on, then comes Asr (late afternoon) prayers. It commences after the end of the time for Zuhr prayers until before sunset. The prayer is made up of 4 raka'ats pre-farz sunnat and 4 raka'at farz prayers. After that come the Maghrib (evening) prayers. The time for this prayer starts immediately after sunset and ends on the fading of twilight. Relative to the other Salat the time duration to offer the Maghrib prayers is short. The prayer consists of 3 raka'at farz prayers, 2 raka'at post-farz sunnat and 2 raka'at nafl prayers. The last prayer of the day is the Isha (early night) prayer. This commences after the fading of twilight and ends before the following dawn but is preferred to be offered before midnight. This prayer consists of 4 raka'ats pre-farz sunnat, 4 raka'ats farz, 2 raka'ats post-farz sunnat, 2 raka'at nafl and 3 raka'at witr prayers.

The raka'at refers to a unit of prayer. The farz raka'ats are compulsory to the performance of the Salat. The sunnat raka'ats are optional but are preferred, though some religious schools differ on the question of offering sunnat prayers. Though strong emphasis is placed on Jama'ah Prayers; Muslims can, nevertheless, perform the five daily prayers on their own on a clean surface, but similar to congregational prayers always facing in the direction of the Ka'bah in Mecca. Muslims must approach the five daily prayers in a state of physical cleanliness. This is achieved through the performance of ablution. In addition to the compulsory five daily prayers there is Salatul Jum'ah or 'Friday Prayers' that are held in congregation.

ZAKAT

Like Salat, the Zakat is an act of worship and obedience – a form of Ibadah. The Zakat can more aptly be described as an annual wealth tax rather than charity. It is the rightful claim of the poor against the rich. It is obligatory upon all Muslims to pay the Zakat who fall within the parameters of wealth specified in various Hadith. The importance of Zakat can be grasped from the following Hadith. Narrated by Abu Ma'bad in Sahih Bukhari, Volume 2, Book 24, Hadith 573: *ALLAH'S Apostle said to Muadh when he sent him to Yemen, "You will go to the people of the Scripture. So, when you reach there, invite them to testify that none has the right to be worshipped but ALLAH, and that Muhammad is His Apostle. And if they obey you in that, tell them that ALLAH has enjoined on them five prayers in each day and night. And if they obey you in that tell them ALLAH has made it obligatory on them to pay the Zakat which will be taken from the rich among them and given to the poor among them. If they obey you in that, then avoid taking the best of their possessions, and be afraid of the curse of an oppressed person because there is no screen between his invocation and ALLAH."*

The concentration and hoarding of wealth in the hands of a few where the majority live in abject poverty is not representative of an Islamic Society. Dire consequences lie in wait for those who do so. This is emphasised in Chapter 3, Al-Imran, Verse 180 of the Holy Qur'an: *"And not let those who hoard up that which ALLAH has bestowed upon them of IIis bounty think that it is good for them. Nay, it is worse for them. That which they hoard will be hung around their necks on the Day of Resurrection. ALLAH's is the heritage of the heavens and the earth: ALLAH is well aware of everything you do."*

The frantic pursuit and hoarding of wealth is forbidden in Islam. This is emphasised in Chapter 9, At-Taubah, Verse 34 of the Holy Qur'an: *"They who hoard up gold and silver and spend it not in the way of ALLAH, unto them give tidings (O Muhammad) of a painful doom."*

In the modern context, gold and silver logically refers to cash in all its manifestations and to land and property, amongst other things.

The Zakat in reality operates as a welfare tax, whereby the well-to-do are encouraged to give voluntarily to the poor. For the most part Zakat is distributed in the month of Ramadan. It is also obligatory on all Muslims on whom Zakat is compulsory to pay Zakat-ul-fitr on the completion of Ramadan but definitely before the Eid-ul-Fitr prayers. This is narrated by Ibn Umar in Sahih Bukhari, Volume 2, Book 25, Hadith 585: *"The Prophet ordered the people to pay Zakat-ul-Fitr before going to the Eid Prayer."*

In addition to Zakat, Muslims who can afford to should also give to charity, called Sadaqa. Furthermore, any personal financial contribution in the way of Islam through the establishments of mosques or madrassahs for instance, though encouraged, is nevertheless, entirely voluntary.

HAJJ

Every Muslim of every nationality yearns to make the pilgrimage to Mecca (perform the Hajj) at least once in their lifetime in spiritual fulfillment of their duty to ALLAH and in observance of one of the Five Pillars of Islam. This is narrated in Chapter 3, Al-Imran, Verses 96-97 of the Holy Qur'an: *"Verily, the first House (of worship) appointed for mankind was that at Mecca, full of blessing, and a guidance for all mankind. In it are manifest signs of ALLAH's guidance; the place where Ibrahim stood up to pray; And whosoever enters it, he attains security. Pilgrimage to the House is a duty mankind owes to ALLAH, -those who can afford the journey. Whosoever disbelieves, (let him know) Lo! ALLAH stands not in need of any of His creatures."*

The Hajj is performed in the twelfth lunar month of the Islamic Calendar between the eight and thirteenth Dhu'l Hijjah. The climax of the Hajj is offering prayers on the plains of Arafat. Muslims believe that it was on this plain where Adam and Eve were reunited and Adam made his covenant with ALLAH. Again the Prophet Muhammad delivered His Farewell Sermon prior to His death from a hillock on the plains of Arafat. It is also where the Prophet Muhammad received the final revelation. The tenth Dhu'l Hijjah marks Eid-ul-Adhar, which is observed across the Globe by Muslims in remembrance of Prophet Ibrahim (Abraham) who was prepared to sacrifice his first and at the time only son - Isma'il (Ishmael) on the command of ALLAH in a trial of Faith.

Through the Hajj all Muslims reaffirm their support in the unity and indivisibility of the Ummah. Irrespective of race, sex or class all pilgrims (between 2-3 million of them) clothed in white pieces of attire assemble for one sole purpose: the worship of the one true God. Among the main Hajj rituals it involves the Tawaf (circumambulation) of the Ka'bah. The Ka'bah, situated in the Al-Masjid Al-Haram (the sacred mosque) serves as the spiritual focal point of Islam. It was through the destruction of the idols housed in the Ka'bah when Muslim forces conquered Mecca under the leadership of the Prophet Muhammad in the month of Ramadan, 8 Al-Hijri (630 AD) that Islam really took hold in Arabia paving the way for the spread of Islam. The triumph over Mecca is referred to as Fateh-e-Mubeen, 'The Glorious Victory'.

SAWM

The Holy Qur'an prescribes for all Muslims, irrespective of race, colour or social standing, fasting in the month of Ramadan, which is the ninth lunar month of the Islamic Calendar. Subject to the sighting of the new Crescent Moon, Ramadan may be for 29 or 30 calendar days. From dawn till dusk able Muslim men and women abstain from food, drink and conjugal relations. The Fast is intended to act as a 'spiritual cleansing' of the physical body and mind. During this month Muslims resign themselves to contemplating in the Divine in submission to ALLAH. Sawm helps to develop taqwa (fear of ALLAH), i.e. self-restraint to overcome worldly desires and evil indulgences drawing oneself nearer to ALLAH. This is narrated in Chapter 2, Al Baqarah, Verse 183 of the Holy Qur'an: *"O ye who believe. Fasting is prescribed for you, as it was prescribed before you, so that you may ward off evil."*

Observing Sawm in the month of Ramadan was specifically mentioned by the Prophet Muhammad in his Farewell Sermon.

The sick are explicitly exempt from fasting during Ramadan. So are travellers' making a journey in that month also exempt. But they must make up for it later in the year while infants are not required to fast. This is mentioned in Chapter 2, Al Baqarah, Verse 185 of the Holy Qur'an: *"The month of*

Ramadan in which was revealed the Quran, a guidance for mankind, and clear proofs of the guidance, and the Criterion (of right and wrong). And whosoever of you is present, let him fast the month, and whosoever of you is sick or on a journey, (let him) fast the same number from other days. ALLAH desireth of you ease; He desireth not hardship for you; and (He desireth) that you should complete the prescribed period, and that ye should magnify ALLAH for having guided you, so that ye may be thankful."

The breaking of the daily Fast after sunset with family and friends followed by the offering of Maghrib prayers is an important highlight of Ramadan. Devotees also perform Tarawih prayers, in addition, to the Isha prayers where very often chapters of the Holy Qur'an are recited. With these prayers usually being held in congregations at local Mosques, Ramadan serves to unite Muslims in a common enterprise achieving a renewed sense of brotherhood and community spirit. The prominence Muslims attach to the Fast is exemplified in the following prayer that is commonly recited when breaking the Fast: *"O ALLAH! I fasted for Thee and I believe in Thee and I put my trust in Thee and with the sustenance Thou hast given me, I now break the fast."*

The month of Ramadan concludes with the celebration of Eid-ul-Fitr. The significance of this day is the Eid-ul-Fitr prayers being offered at Mosques across the Muslim Ummah that are usually held in the mornings and in congregation. All Heads of State and Heads of Government of every Muslim majority State will also offer these prayers in congregation. Muslims will exchange Eid Greetings with one another and visit family and friends putting aside differences. The Eid therefore, serves to cement bonds of brotherhood and friendship.

The month of Ramadan is of immense significance in the hearts and minds of Muslims. It was during this month on the night termed Lailatul Qadr (Night of Power) that the Holy Qur'an was first revealed to the Prophet Muhammad marking the beginning of His prophetic mission. It was also during Ramadan that Mecca was conquered under the leadership of the Prophet Muhammad whereby the Ka'bah was cleansed of idols. Consequently, idol worship was banished and Arabia liberated itself from pagan worship.

It is clear that the Five Pillars of Islam have one underlying theme at their core, namely unity of the Muslim Ummah in submission to the worship of the one true GOD. While the First Pillar relates to Shahadah, i.e. declaration of faith in Tauhid and the Risalah of Muhammad the remaining Four Pillars relate to Ibadah, i.e. actions performed to gain ALLAH's favour.

SEVEN ARTICLES OF FAITH

Complementing the Five Pillars of Islam are the Seven Articles of Faith. In expressing their faith in the Shahadah (declaration of Faith) it is imperative for Muslims to profess their belief in the Seven Articles of Faith. This Declaration of Faith is narrated in Al-Imanul Mufassal as follows: *"I believe in ALLAH, in His angels, in His books, in His messengers, in the Last Day [Day of Judgement] and in the fact that everything good or bad is decided by ALLAH the Almighty, and in the life-after-death."*

BELIEF IN THE ONENESS OF ALLAH

Belief in the oneness and unity of ALLAH invokes the doctrine of Tauhid, which has been discussed at some length earlier in the introduction. Muslims believe that there is no God but ALLAH and all worship is due to ALLAH alone. Muslims do not associate partners with ALLAH for that is shirk (unpardonable sin).

BELIEF IN THE ANGELS OF ALLAH

Muslims are required to believe in the angels of ALLAH. They are created from Nur (Divine Light) for the purpose of serving ALLAH, the vast majority of them being tasked with specific functions. Man, on the other hand, is created from clay and has been given free will, unlike the angels. The Jinn are created from smokeless fire, including Iblis (the Devil). It is commonly misunderstood that Iblis was an angel himself and their leader. On the contrary, Iblis was the most prominent among the Jinn who fell from ALLAH's Grace after failing to prostrate before Adam on ALLAH's command and therefore, banished from Heaven. This is narrated in Chapter 18, Al-Kahf, verse 50: *"Behold! We said to the angels, "Prostrate To Adam": they prostrated except Iblis, He was one of the Jinns, and he broke the Command Of his Lord. Will ye then take him and his progeny as protectors Rather than Me? And they are enemies to you! Evil would be the exchange for the wrong-doers!"*

Again in Chapter 7, Al-A'raf verses 12-18 it states: *"(ALLAH) said: "What prevented thee (Iblis) from prostrating when I commanded thee?" He said: "I am better than he: Thou didst create me from fire, and him from clay". ALLAH said: "Get thee down hence, it is not for thee to be arrogant here: get out, for thou art of the meanest (of creatures)." He (Iblis) said: "Give me respite till the day they are raised up." ALLAH said: "Be thou among those who have respite." He (Iblis) said: "Because thou hast thrown me out, lo I will lie in wait for them on Thy Straight Way: "Then will I assault them from before them and behind them, from their right and their left: Nor wilt Thou find, in most of them, Gratitude (for Thy mercies)." ALLAH said: "Get out from this, despised and expelled. If any of them follow thee,- Hell will I fill with you all."*

Prominent among the angels is Jibra'il (Gabriel) who is the Archangel and brought the revelation from ALLAH to Muhammad and the other Rasuls (Messengers). Another important angel is Azra'il, also known as Malakul Mawt (angel of death) and is responsible for ending our life on earth by removing ours souls from our physical bodies. Again there is the angel Israfil who is tasked with the job of blowing the trumpet at the end of time that will herald in the Day of Judgement. Having no free will, angels are incapable of committing sin. Jinn similar to Man, on the other hand, are capable of free will to choose between good and evil. They are tempted to commit sin through the evil whispers of Iblis and his minions. Both Man and Jinn therefore, seek refuge with ALLAH to overcome these evil temptations. This is narrated in Chapter 114 of the Holy Qur'an: *"Say I seek refuge in the Lord of Mankind, The King of mankind, The God of mankind, From the evil of the sneaking whisperer, who whispereth in the hearts of mankind, of the jinn and of mankind."*

BELIEF IN THE DIVINE REVELATIONS

This Article of Faith requires Muslims to believe in all the Divine revelations, i.e. the Tawrat (Torah) revealed to the Prophet Musa (Moses); the Zabur (Psalms) revealed to the Prophet Dawud (David); the Injil (the original Gospel) revealed to the Prophet Isa (Jesus) and the Qur'an revealed to the final Prophet and Messenger Muhammad. However, the Divine revelations preceding the Holy Qur'an are believed by Muslims to have been lost, corrupted, forgotten, neglected and even concealed by Man, whether it was for the furtherance of political ambition or religious orthodoxy. The Uthmanic Codex, on the other hand, has remained unaltered for the last fourteen hundred years being compiled within only 20 years of the Prophet Muhammad's death. In Islam the Holy Qur'an therefore, takes precedence over the preceding Divine Texts to the extent of any inconsistencies between them.

BELIEF IN THE MESSENGERS OF ALLAH

As a part of their Faith, Muslims must believe in all the Prophets and Messengers of ALLAH. The Holy Qur'an mentions 25 of the most prominent Prophets by name. ALLAH has sent Prophets and Messengers to all nations at different times. This is narrated in Chapter 10, Yunus, verse 47 of the Holy Qur'an where it states: *"To every nation (was sent) a Messenger: when their Messenger comes (before them), the matter will be judged between them with Justice, and they will not be wronged."*

It must be reiterated that the Prophet Muhammad was sent to all mankind and is the last prophet and messenger till the end of time. Muhammad is proclaimed by ALLAH as the last of the chain of the true Prophet, "Khatam-an-Nabiyyin". All the Prophets preached worship and submission to the one true God. Four of the prophets mentioned in the Holy Qur'an were sent with books of guidance. As mentioned above they are the Prophet Musa (Moses); the Prophet Dawud (David); the Prophet Isa (Jesus) and the final Prophet and Messenger Muhammad. It must be emphasised that from the point of view that Jews, Christians and Muslims believe in true monotheism they are brothers in Faith.

BELIEF IN THE DAY OF RESURRECTION/RECKONING/JUDGEMENT

Muslims are required to believe in the Day of Judgment. It is when all Mankind will stand before their Lord in judgement for their actions on earth. This is stated in Chapter 83, Al-Mutaffifinn, verse 6: *"The day when (all) mankind stand before the Lord of the Worlds."*

Everyone will be judged on their each and every action as narrated in Chapter 99, Az-Zalzalah, verses 7-8: *"And whoso doeth good an atom's weight will see it then, and whoso doeth ill an atom's weight will see it then."*

ALLAH warns Mankind in Chapter 82, Al-Infitar, verse 19 that the Day of Judgment will belong to ALLAH alone. Mankind will be helpless that Day: *"A day on which no soul hath power at all for any (other) soul. The (absolute) command on that day is ALLAH's."*

A study of Chapters 83 and 84 of the Holy Qur'an also gives further insight on the Day of Reckoning. Everything we do in this worldly life, every intention we have, every thought we entertain, and every word we say, are all recorded. On the Day of Judgment they will be revealed. People with good records will be generously rewarded and warmly welcomed to the Heaven of God, and those with bad records will be punished and cast into hellfire.

BELIEF IN LIFE AFTER DEATH

The belief that there is life after death forms the cornerstone of all the three monotheist religions, for upon this belief hinges the concept of Heaven and Hell, i.e. reward and punishment for one's actions on Earth. Throughout the ages, Prophets and

Messengers have been sent inviting people to Paradise and warning them against giving in to evil indulgences that leads to hellfire. Closely intertwined with the Islamic belief of life after death is the fact that all mankind will stand in judgement before ALLAH. Belief in an afterlife gives respite to those who fear ALLAH and observe the religious tenets of Islam, especially those who are oppressed and persecuted. For the God fearing, the belief that life on Earth is temporary and life after death is eternal provides solace to the soul. It should not, however, form the basis of satisfying oneself with a sense of revenge against the evildoers. As Muslims it is our duty to invite wrongdoers to the path of Islam rather than be complaisant to their actions, eager that they will end up in hellfire.

BELIEF IN PREDESTINATION

Referred to as Al-Qadr, predestination requires all Muslims to believe that events take place according to the exact Knowledge of ALLAH. They include the creation of the Universe with the single command: "Be!" as well as the destiny of mankind. Whether or not the Universe was created from nothing, it transpired on the direction of ALLAH. Everything that has resulted from that 'Act of Creation' is within the realm of Divine Knowledge and control. ALLAH has also given mankind free will to make choices and decisions, but these are limited to our finite nature. Some view this article of predestination as defeatist, implying that the poor in society must accept their station in life as fate. But this is a misinterpretation. ALLAH has given us vast opportunities to realize our full potential, but it is our mismanagement of resources that has led to disparity of wealth.

CHAPTER FOUR

Muhammad – "the Seal of the Prophets"

You could be forgiven for thinking that Muhammad was a myth; such was the grand scale of His many achievements and personal attributes. Surely He was a man, but no ordinary man. His persona eclipses the likes of Alexander the Great in terms of military genius and Aristotle in terms of wisdom. He was an unparalleled social reformer, an intense lover and devoted father. This chapter reflects on the personal pains and stresses Muhammad endured in His early years and some of the momentous events that mark His Prophethood. I have also briefly touched upon the significance of the Prophet's Ahadith and the controversy surrounding their collection.

MUHAMMAD'S EARLY YEARS

To describe Muhammad's early life as tragic is an understatement, but Muslims must accept this as the will of

ALLAH and part of ALLAH's scheme of things in His grand design. Muhammad was born in Mecca into the powerful tribe of the Quraysh in the year 570 AD. His father Abdullah, son of Abd al-Muttalib, died when Muhammad was still in His mother's womb. Muhammad's mother, Aminah bint Wahb died when He was only six years old. Muhammad was therefore orphaned at a very early age and deprived of the love and affection of His parents.

A few years after His birth and during the lifetime of His mother Aminah, Muhammad was entrusted to a Bedouin foster-mother, Halimah al-Sa'diyyah, it being the custom then for Arab tribes such as the Quraysh to have their newborn babies cared for and nursed by foster mothers. Tradition has it that during His stay with His foster parents the young Muhammad while playing with His foster brothers was seized upon by two Angels who appeared as men in white who cleansed His heart with what appeared to be snow. The spiritual message conveyed by this incident is that Muhammad was destined to be no ordinary man but the Beloved of ALLAH, chosen to convey the Divine Message to Humanity for eternity.

Following the death of His mother, His paternal grandfather, Abd al-Muttalib of the Hashimite Clan and a leading figure in Mecca, cared for Muhammad. But Abd al-Muttalib soon passed away and it was Muhammad's Uncle and later protector, Abu Talib, who reared Him to adulthood. Abu Talib was a respected leader of the Quraysh and a successful merchant, but more significantly he was the father of Ali (Muhammad's son-in-law and the fourth Rashidun Caliph). In addition to being a shepherd boy minding sheep, Muhammad at the age of 12 accompanied His uncle on a trade journey to Syria. This trip is viewed with significance as Muslim Tradition holds that during this trip a Nestorian Monk, called Bahirah, based on his keen observation of the young boy, predicted that Muhammad was going to be a prophet in the future. Muslim tradition therefore holds that during Muhammad's early years there were indications that Muhammad was destined to lead an extraordinary life.

In Mecca as a young man, Muhammad was known as al-Amin, 'the trustworthy'. He inspired confidence in others due to his sincerity, honesty, integrity and strength of character. It was because of these personal attributes that Muhammad, then aged 25, was called upon by a wealthy female merchant called Khadijah bint al-Khuwaylid to take a caravan to Syria. This would result in a dramatic turn of events for Muhammad, not only for His personal life but also for His Prophetic mission. So impressed was Khadijah with Muhammad's commission and the reports from her manservant Maysara who accompanied Muhammad on the expedition that she proposed marriage to Him. This Muhammad accepted. Khadijah was older than Muhammad at the time of the marriage; tradition has it 15 years older. She was a widower having lost two previous husbands. But she was intelligent, wealthy and loved Muhammad not least for His reputation in Mecca, but also by His good character and truthfulness.

They had six children together, two sons, Qasim and Abdullah (who both died in infancy) as well as four daughters, including Fatimah, who married Ali; they became the proud parents of Hasan and Husayn. (In the second civil war that engulfed the Caliphate, Husayn and his family were murdered at Karbala.) Muhammad's marriage to Khadijah was not intended by Him to be one of economic convenience. Far from it, Muhammad made no personal gain for Himself from Khadijah's wealth but instead gave alms to the poor from the family income and continued to be a merchant, leading a simple life.

Muhammad never remarried while Khadijah was still alive. He was a devoted husband and a loving father to His children. The Prophet Muhammad was no sexual predator, as has been alleged over the years by extreme right wing opponents and some feminist groups.

As the years went by, Muhammad's standing in Mecca steadily grew, and He was often called upon to arbitrate in matters of dispute. On one such occasion, prior to His Prophethood, Muhammad's prowess came to light. With the Ka'bah falling into a state of disrepair, the Quraysh had taken the decision to rebuild portions of it. However, bitter infighting soon developed among the Clans, threatening to break the fragile unity of the Quraysh about which Clan should have the honour of positioning the Black Stone. (Tradition has it that initially the Stone was white and had been sent down to Earth as a gift/sign from Heaven.) Muhammad, then in His mid-thirties, was called to arbitrate. Considering the context of the situation, in what can be described as nothing short of brilliance, Muhammad advised that the Black Stone should be placed in the centre of a cloak with a representative of each Clan holding the edges of the cloak and jointly lifting the Stone into place. This solution preserved the unity of the Clans in this noble enterprise.

Despite the modest comforts of His everyday life, Muhammad became increasingly disturbed by the malaise in Mecca, with its idol worship, prevailing social injustice, economic exploitation, disparity of wealth and self-destructing tribal feuds. This state of affairs is referred to as Jahiliyyah (pre-Islamic ignorance). Muhammad would seek answers to this chaos by resorting to mountain retreats. It was during one of these retreats in the month of Ramadan, in around 610 AD, that

Muhammad, then aged forty, underwent an extra-ordinary experience that marked the first of a series of Divine Revelations that continued for the next 23 years of His Prophetic life culminating in the Holy Qur'an. (This is discussed in more detail in Chapter 1).

There was nothing new about the revelations received by Prophet Muhammad. The Holy Qur'an confirms the Holy Books that preceded it namely, the Zabur (Psalms) revealed to Prophet Dawud (David), the Tawrat (Torah) revealed to Prophet Musa (Moses) and the Injil (the original Gospel) revealed to Prophet Isa (Jesus). The monotheist religions all have one central theme at their core: the worship of the one true God. The Holy Qur'an does, however, disassociate itself from the subsequent corruption and distortions that later found their way into the preceding Revealed Books as narrated in Chapter 5, Al-Ma'idah, verse 13-16: *"Because they broke their Covenant, so We distanced them (from Us) and hardened their hearts. They distort the meaning of the (revealed) words and have forgotten some of what they were told to remember; you (Prophet) will always find treachery in all but a few of them. Overlook this and pardon them: ALLAH loves those who are kind. We also took a Covenant from those who say, 'We are Christians,' But they too forgot some of what they were told to remember, so We stirred up enmity and hatred among them until the Day of Resurrection, when ALLAH will tell them what they have done. People of the Book! Our Messenger has come to make clear to you much of what you have kept hidden of the Scripture, and to overlook much [you have done]. A light has now come to you from ALLAH, and a Scripture making things clear, with which ALLAH guides to the ways of peace those who follow what pleases Him, bringing them from darkness out into light, by His will, and guiding them to a straight path."*

The Divine Texts preceding the Holy Qur'an were

compromised to further the political and religious establishment that later followed.

THE BATTLE OF BADR: A DECISIVE VICTORY

Incensed by the increasing number of converts to Islam and consequently, the threat Muhammad posed to the Meccan socio-political order, Muslims were increasingly being persecuted by the ruling elite in Mecca. The vast majority of them had no choice but to escape literally with their lives. In their haste they were forced to leave behind much of their wealth and possessions. Muhammad and his Sahabah (closest companions) were among the last to make their escape. They chose to migrate to the city of Yathrib (later renamed Medinatun Nabi or Medina). Their decision to migrate was inspired by the second Pledge of Aqaba made in 622 AD. This flight from persecution is referred to as the Hijrah.

In turn the ruling Quraysh in Mecca confiscated the belongings that the Muslims had left behind. This inevitably caused resentment among the exiled Muslims against their former Meccan rulers. But then Medina was strategically placed on the caravan-trading route between Mecca and Syria, and Mecca was desperate to secure her trading routes. Discontent was at boiling point. Full-scale armed engagement was inevitable. But the Prophet Muhammad refrained from armed attack. This stance He maintained until He received a revelation invoking Muslims permission to fight. This is narrated in Chapter 22, Al-Hajj, verse 39: *"To those against whom war is made, sanction is given (to fight), because they have been wronged: - And verily, ALLAH is indeed able to give them victory."*

It must be emphasised here that the Prophet was not a man

who actively sought bloodshed. He was not a man of the sword, as some right-wing propagandists, and for that matter so-called Islamic extremists, have made Him out to be. Far from it, during the 10-plus years the Prophet preached in Mecca, Muslims were forbidden to fight their Meccan persecutors despite the many transgressions directed against the Muslim community. Armed strife with the Meccans from within Mecca would definitely have meant annihilation for the small community of Muslims.

Forced into exile along with His many fellow Muslims, the Prophet changed tack. He now had permission to fight in the cause of ALLAH. As events unfolded Muhammad proved to be a brilliant strategist. He seized the initiative to bring the trading routes to and from Mecca under His control. To impress the message to the Meccan rulers that trade caravans passing near Medina now faced serious danger, the Prophet dispatched raiding parties periodically to ambush caravans travelling along the main commercial trading routes in and out of Mecca.

As chance would have it, in 624 AD, a large caravan was making its way from Syria to Mecca headed by Abu Sufyan. He was Chief of the Banu Abd-Shams Clan of the Quraysh tribe, making him one of the most powerful rulers of Mecca. A small force of only 313 ill-equipped Muslims set out to meet the caravan under the command of the Prophet Muhammad. They camped at the wells of Badr. Fearing an attack from the Muslims, Abu Sufyan sent message to Mecca to come to his aid. The Meccans rulers responded by assembling a large fighting force of more than 1000 well-equipped men, including 100 horses and a large number of camels. They began their march to Badr.

In the meantime, Abu Sufyan changed the route of his caravan out of reach of the Muslims. He then sent message that the trade caravan was safe and advised that the Meccan Force should return back. Those commanding the Meccan Force refused to accept this advice, for this was their opportunity to crush the Muslims once and for all and they would do so in battle, or so they thought, particularly Abu Jahl. He viewed this as an opportunity to consolidate his position in Mecca as the ruler who subdued the Muslims. But as it transpired, they all underestimated the religious zeal of the Muslim Force.

As regards the two ill-matched Forces, the Holy Qur'an narrates this in Chapter 3, Al-Imran, Verse 13: *"There has already been for you a Sign in the two armies that met (in combat); One army was fighting in the Cause of ALLAH; and the other made up of disbelievers. With their own eyes (the former) saw (the latter) to be twice their own numbers, but ALLAH strengtheneth with His succour whom He wills. Herein verily is a lesson for all with eyes to see."*

The Prophet Muhammad strategically placed His men by the wells of Badr, which meant that the Quraysh would have to fight for water. Prior to the Battle, conditions were imposed by the Prophet upon the Muslim fighters on rules of armed engagement. Women were not to be harmed, nor were children or old people. No harm was to be done to men who worked in the field. Orders were given that trees should not be cut down. Muslims were ordered only to strike against those who had expelled them and enriched themselves with their possessions.

In keeping with battle tradition, the battle of Badr too began with single combat, with both sides producing their champions. Hamzah, Ali and Ubaydah ibn al-Harith represented the Muslims, while Utba, Shayba and al-Walid ibn Utba represented the Meccan Force. The Meccan champions did not stand a chance against the likes of Hamzah and Ali. Utba, the father of Hind, who was the wife of Abu Sufyan, was brought down by Hamzah, while Utba's son, al-Walid (Hinds brother), was killed by Ali's sword.

Soon after this the Battle began in earnest. The Muslims fighting that day clearly understood that this was a make or break situation for them. Defeat would mean certain death for all of them. The Meccans were in no mood to take prisoners. For the Muslims their backs were against the wall. It was a kill or be killed scenario.

The situation as it presented itself to the Muslim Force was an extremely desperate one. Defeat was not an option. What started out to be a raid on Abu Sufyan's caravan transpired to be a battle of survival for the religion of Islam. And the Prophet Muhammad knew it. Inspired by religious zeal, however, the Muslims fought with discipline and vigour. Many former Muslim slaves found themselves fighting their one-time Meccan masters on an equal footing, and fighting to the death. By midday the Meccan force, despite regrouping themselves a number of times, finally had to flee in disarray, leaving many prominent Meccans dead on the battlefield, including Abu Jahl. The Meccans had clearly underestimated the Muslim force in its ability to execute an effective battle strategy.

So decisive was the Battle of Badr that it is mentioned in the Holy Qur'an. In Chapter 3, Al-Imran, Verse 123 it states: *"ALLAH had helped you at Badr, when you were Helpless; Then be mindful of ALLAH, so that you may be grateful."*

With regard to the Meccan war captives, they were handled with remarkable mercy. Inspired by Revelation, the Prophet Muhammad adopted a humane policy towards them. The captives were not to be ill-treated in any way. Many of the captives were close relatives of Muslims. Those who could pay a ransom were freed. The poor and old were freed without ransom. Those captives who could read and write were charged with teaching Muslims in order to gain their freedom. This humane and tolerant treatment brought dividends, as many captives voluntarily converted to Islam.

Lessons can certainly be learnt from this. Once victory is realised, vengeance should not be actively pursued. Rather efforts should be taken to exemplify the truth of your beliefs, establishing moral ascendancy over your opponent.

If the Prophet Muhammad's enemies considered Him a spent force that could be brushed aside with relative ease, the victory at the wells of Badr changed all that. The Prophet was now a man to be reckoned with. No more was He a Meccan exile but instead a major leader of the Hijaz. The success at Badr also enhanced His position in Medina, allowing Him to subdue His opponents there. These were the Jewish Tribes of Banu Qainuqa, Banu Nadir and Banu Quraiza. Not only did they stand accused of spreading discontent in Medina against the Prophet, they also plotted to kill Him. The tribe of Banu Quraiza went as far as conspiring with the Meccan army in 627 AD during the Battle of the Ditch in a siege that almost brought down Medina. This was despite the fact that they pledged themselves to the Constitution of Medina.

The deaths of many of the Meccan ruling elite at Badr helped to consolidate Abu Sufyan's position as the undisputed leader of Mecca. It therefore became imperative upon him to seek military engagement with the Muslims. Naturally the Meccans sought retribution for their humiliating defeat at the wells of Badr. More so, Hind had a death-score to settle with Hamzah, the man who killed her father, Utba. Battle preparations were made in earnest, with Meccans calling upon Bedouin tribes to join them in their war against the Muslims. History records that the Meccans exacted their revenge in the Battle of Uhud in 625 AD.

THE CONQUEST OF MECCA:
THE TURNING POINT

In 628 AD, in the sixth year of the Hijrah, the Prophet Muhammad set out for the Ka'bah with around 1400 unarmed Muslims to perform Umra (short pilgrimage). Notwithstanding their defeat in the Battle of Uhud, the Muslims in Medina were emboldened after the subsequent abortive Meccan Siege in what came to be known as the Battle of the Ditch, despite being overwhelmed by the enemy's superior numbers of 10,000 men. The Muslims must surely have felt that ALLAH was on their side. Dressed in their white pilgrimage attire, they approached Mecca, stopping at Hudaibiyah. It was a tactical move on behalf of the Prophet, for He knew that the Quraysh as guardians of the Ka'bah would not slaughter unarmed pilgrims, as this would cause outrage among the tribes and nomads of Arabia. But then it was also unlikely that the Meccans would simply allow Muslims to enter Mecca, for that would surely amount to severe humiliation on their part. Plans were therefore put into effect to prevent this. Khalid bin al-Walid (Khalid) was dispatched with a Force to stop the Muslims from entering Mecca. What followed was an intense standoff. Consequently, an agreement was reached between the Quraysh and the Prophet. This agreement has come to be known as the Hudaibiyah Agreement.

The conditions in this agreement would in turn set the stage for the conquest of Mecca, although it did not appear so at the time of signing. In fact, so disheartened were the Prophet's Companions with this agreement that it risked mutiny. The conditions of the Hudaibiyah Agreement were that Prophet Muhammad and His followers would return to Medina without performing the Umra at the Ka'bah on that occasion (thereby saving face for the rulers of Mecca). But the next year Muslims would return to Mecca as pilgrims and remain for no more than three days to perform the religious rites of the Umra around the Ka'bah unhindered. Furthermore, members of the Quraysh who had become Muslims and emigrated to Medina would be returned to Mecca on demand. But no such reciprocity applied to the Quraysh in respect of Muslims taking refuge in Mecca.

There would also be a truce for 10 years between Mecca and Medina. Muslims could go to Mecca and Ta'if, while the Quraysh could make trips to Syria through Muslim areas. Each party would remain neutral in the event of a war between the other and a third party. The Bedouin tribes were free to choose to make an alliance with either Mecca or Medina. Finally, as part of the truce neither party could attack any tribe nor ambush any caravan or injure any individual associated with either of them. Breach of the truce would render the agreement void.

What really incensed the Prophet's closest Companions was that the truce meant that Muslims could no longer raid the Quraysh trade caravans, in effect ending the economic blockade of Mecca. Further cause for humiliation was when the Prophet Muhammad waived any reference in the Hudaibiyah Agreement of Himself as the Messenger of ALLAH but instead as the son of Abdullah.

The Prophet however was understandably keen to establish a truce with Mecca. He did not want further battles or bloodletting with them, but more importantly He wanted to gain access to the Ka'bah. This would allow for a propaganda strategy in winning the hearts and minds of the Meccans. Crucially, with the agreement allowing Bedouin tribes to form alliances with Medina, abandoning their old alliances with the

Quraysh, the Banu Khuza'ah sided with the Muslims. The Banu Bakr, on the other hand, who were antagonistic towards Banu Khuza'ah, remained with the Quraysh. Significantly, soon after the Hudaibiyah Agreement, many non-Muslims embraced Islam, including Khaled. He would later prove to be an asset as a military strategist and commander.

In November of 629 AD, one of the clans of Banu Bakr launched a surprise night-time attack on Banu Khuza'ah in their own territory, allegedly with the aid and assistance of the Quraysh. Though members of the Banu Khuza'ah took refuge in the sacred precincts of the Ka'bah, they were still butchered there. This single incident would ignite a storm across Arabia, resulting in the surrender of Mecca.

The Banu Khuza'ah appealed to the Prophet. Realising that the Hudaibiyah agreement lay in tatters and that the Prophet would respond by seizing this opportunity to His advantage, Abu Sufyan hastily went to Medina to plead with the Prophet Muhammad that the truce was still in force. But the damage was already done. The conditions of the Hudaibiyah Agreement were breached and the Truce was now void. Realising that the balance of power was about to change in the Hijaz many other tribal leaders pledged their allegiance to the Prophet.

In January 630 AD, in the month of Ramadan, in the eighth year of the Hijrah, the Prophet Muhammad set off for Mecca at the head of a large force numbering more than 10,000 men. The Quraysh had no means of repelling such a large Muslim army. Mecca had no alternative but to capitulate to the Muslim Force. The Meccans feared that the Muslim army would enter Mecca and exact a revenge that would result in a bloodbath. Realising this, Abu Sufyan made his way to the Muslim Camp, which was just a few miles away from Mecca. Upon embracing Islam, he left for Mecca to warn its inhabitants of the impending massacre that he believed would befall them, despite a promise to the contrary by the Prophet Muhammad. In fear of their survival the Quraysh barricaded themselves indoors. Approaching Mecca from all directions, the Muslim Force, however, entered Mecca without incident. The Prophet Muhammad declared a general amnesty. Despite having been ridiculed, persecuted and finally forced into exile eight years before, the Prophet did not exact vengeance. It was not His purpose to do so. His principal objective was to cleanse the Ka'bah of the idols housed in it. To the deafening cries of ALLAHU AKBAR (ALLAH is the Greatest), the Prophet Muhammad smashed the idols placed in and around the Ka'bah. With this definitive act of defiance against the old order, paganism and idolatry were banished from Arabia.

With the conquest of Mecca, again the Prophet proved that He was not a man of the sword. Despite having the opportunity to crush His Meccan persecutors and put an end to potential rivals, the Prophet ordered His Muslim army not to exact revenge. No one was to be harmed and no closed doors were to be forced. By commanding so, the victory over Mecca was permanent. Having consolidated His power over Mecca and Medina, the stage was set for the banner of Islam to spread across the Hijaz and beyond the Arabian Peninsula.

In hindsight, the Prophet's decision not to avenge His former enemies proved to be a disastrous oversight in the context of the subsequent Fitna (civil wars) that engulfed the Caliphate after His death. For it was Abu Sufyan's son Mu'awiya who founded the Umayyad Dynasty and whose successive caliphs ruled the expanding Islamic Empire between 661 till 750 AD. Crucially, it was Mu'awiya's son Yazid I who upon succeeding his father as Caliph, orchestrated the massacre of the Prophet's grandson

Husayn, together with his family, at Karbala in 680 AD. Consequently this effectively brought to an end any claim by the Hashemite Clan, i.e., Prophet's immediate household and blood relatives to the Caliphate. This murderous affair also marks the principal schism between Muslims that has persisted throughout the ages namely, that of Shi'ite and Sunni Islam, and continues today. This is discussed in more detail in Chapter 5.

HADITH AND ISLAM

The Hadith narrate the actual sayings and actions of the Prophet Muhammad. With numerous collections of Ahadith (plural for hadith) being undertaken during the second century Al Hijri, six collections have been widely regarded by Muslims through the ages as being authoritative, with two of them being regarded as authentic in their entirety. They are the Sahih al-Bukhari (collected and compiled by Abu Abdallah Muhammad bin Isma'il al-Bukhari) and Sahih al-Muslim (collected and compiled by Muslim ibn al-Hajjaj). The other four collections, though held in high esteem, are not recognised as authentic in their entirety. These four collections of Hadith are the Sunan Abu Dawud, Sunan Ibn Majah, Jami At-Tirmidhi and Sunan An-Nasa'i.

The importance attached by the Muslim world to these six authoritative collections should not be underestimated, for after the Holy Qur'an the Ahadith are the principal source of Shari'ah law, customs and practices. On many important issues the Holy Qur'an simply states the principles while it is the Ahadith that provides details of their application. For example, while the Holy Qur'an requires Muslims to offer Salah, observe sawm and pay zakat it does not specify the manner and form by which these are to be carried out. It is from the Sunnah of the Prophet Muhammad that we derive the details. This is narrated in Chapter 16, An-Nahl, verse 44 of the Holy Al Qur'an: *"(We sent them) with Clear Signs and Scriptures. And we have sent down the Message unto thee (Prophet) too; That thou mayest explain clearly to men what is sent for them, that they may reflect."*

Unlike the verses of the Holy Qur'an that were compiled into a single volume within a few years of the Prophet Muhammad's death, the Ahadith were collected more than 200 years after His death. Given the long period of oral transmission before the Hadiths came to be written down and collected, it is alleged by critics that there was every possibility that some of the Hadiths mingled fact and myth, truth and error into one big melting pot. Furthermore, with the ongoing power struggles within the Caliphate there was a real opportunity for spurious Hadiths to support rival positions, schisms and grievances. Notwithstanding this, the scholars engaged in collecting the Hadith went to great lengths in establishing the reliability of the chain of transmitters. In fact, an entire science thoroughly investigating the character and background of each transmitter to identify the strength and weakness of the chain of transmitters was developed. Consequently, the numerous Hadiths were graded into varying degrees of reliability in terms of trustworthiness of the sources, multiple references and the chain of verbal succession, among other things. The grades are sahih (sound), hasan (good) and daif (weak). This obsession with examining the chain often overshadows the importance of taking into account the content of the numerous Hadith and their compatibility with the Holy Qur'an.

THE FAREWELL SERMON

In 632 AD, in the 10th year of the Hijrah, leading a large number of pilgrims, the Prophet Muhammad set out for Mecca from Medina to perform the annual Hajj. Sadly, this would turn out to be the Prophet's last pilgrimage. The rituals set down in the Prophet's farewell pilgrimage form the established rituals of the Hajj. On completion of the Farewell Hajj the Prophet, believing that His death was near, took the opportunity of addressing the Ummah on the plains of Arafat to surmise His Prophetic Message in what has come to be known as the Farewell Sermon. It must be remembered that the Farewell Sermon is not Divine Revelation comparable to the verses of the Holy Qur'an. Nevertheless, its impact on the Muslim Psyche cannot be underestimated.

Praising and thanking ALLAH, the Prophet said:

"Oh people, listen to my words carefully for I know not whether I will meet you on such an occasion again."

"Oh people, just as you regard this month, this day, this city as sacred, so regard the life and property of every Muslim as a sacred trust. Remember that you will indeed appear before God and answer for your actions."

"Return the things kept with you as trust (Amanah) to their rightful owners."

"All dues of interest shall stand cancelled and you will have only your capital back. ALLAH has forbidden interest, and I cancel the dues of interest payable to my uncle Abbas ibn Abdul Muttalib."

"Oh people, your wives have certain rights over you and you have certain rights over them. Treat them well and be kind to them for they are your committed partners and committed helpers."

"Beware of Satan, he is desperate to divert you from the worship of

ALLAH so beware of him in matters of your way of life."

"Oh people, listen carefully! Let all your feuds be abolished. All the believers are brothers. You are not allowed to the things belonging to another Muslim unless he gives it to you willingly."

"Oh people, you are all descended from Adam and none is higher than the other except in obedience to ALLAH. No Arab is superior to a non-Arab. Between Muslims there are no races and no tribes. Do not oppress and do not be oppressed."

"Oh people, reflect on my words. I leave behind two things, the Qur'an, revealed by ALLAH which is light and guidance and my example and if you follow these, you will not fail."

"Listen to me carefully! Worship ALLAH and offer Salah; observe Sawm in the month of Ramadan; pay the Zakah and perform the Hajj."

"Oh people, be mindful of those who work under you. Feed and clothe them as you feed and clothe yourselves."

"Oh people, no prophet or messenger will come after me and no new faith will emerge."

"All those who listen to me shall pass on my words to others and those to others again."

The Prophet Muhammad then asked the multitude of people assembled, *"Have I conveyed the Message of ALLAH to you, Oh People?"* The tens of thousands that had gathered answered in one voice, "You have, and ALLAH is the witness." As the Prophet finished delivering His sermon the following revelation came to Him as narrated in Chapter 5, Al-Ma'idah, verse 3: *"Today I have perfected your religion for you, completed my favour upon you and have chosen for you Islam as your religion."*

Against the backdrop of an Arabia plagued with tribal allegiances and blood feuds, the Farewell Sermon was nothing short of revolutionary, for it tore away at divisive tribal allegiances that had formed the bedrock of Arabia, reiterating that all Muslims were part of the same one Ummah and united in faith. While Muslims are reminded not to be persecuted, at the same time, they are warned not to transgress. The Sermon's emphasis on the status of spouses, that they both have rights and obligations to one another, was a radical departure from the norm at the time. Emphasis was also put on treating the weak in society with compassion. To truly appreciate the magnificence of the Farewell Sermon with respect to social reform it is worthwhile noting that it was delivered in the context of the seventh century, when Arabia was only just emerging from Jahiliyyah (pre-Islamic ignorance), when Europe was sunk in the Dark Ages and when old empires were crumbling.

PROPHET MUHAMMAD: KHATAM-AN-NABIYYIN

The Prophet Muhammad is the last of ALLAH's Apostles. He is referred to as Khatam-an-Nabiyyin (the seal of prophethood). No Messenger will appear after Him. No new monotheist Faith will emerge after Islam. The Prophet makes this clear in His Farewell Sermon. Further, the Holy Qur'an in Chapter 33, Al-Azhab, verse 40 narrates: *"Muhammad is not the father of any of your men, but (he is) The Messenger of ALLAH and the Seal of the Prophets: and ALLAH has full knowledge of all things."*

What distinguishes Muhammad from the other preceding Prophets is that while they were sent to a chosen people/nation, Muhammad was sent by ALLAH to all mankind as stated in Chapter 34, Saba, verse 28: *"We have not sent thee (Muhammad) But as a Messenger to all mankind, giving them Glad tidings, and warning them (Against sin), but most men know not."*

With the Message of Islam being universal in its appeal, it is only natural that the Messenger communicating the Divine Message should be the universal Prophet. Furthermore, of the Divine Books, the Holy Qur'an is the last of the Divine Revelations. Again ALLAH makes a covenant with Mankind through Muhammad by revealing to the Prophet that Islam is the chosen religion as narrated in Chapter 5, Al-Ma'idah, verse 3 above. This narrative is further supported in Chapter 48, Al-Fath, Verse 28: *"It was He Who sent His Messenger with Guidance and the Religion of Truth, to make it show that it is above all (other) religions. ALLAH suffices as a Witness."*

From a political perspective, in the interest of maintaining unity and integrity in the Ummah, it was imperative that the Prophet Muhammad was clearly accepted and firmly established as the last of the chain of the true Prophets in accordance with Divine revelation. This would act as a natural deterrent on false apostasy claims. Nevertheless, shortly after the Prophet Muhammad's death Abu Bakr spent most of his time as Caliph battling against false Prophets in what has come to be known as the Apostasy wars and won. The false prophets included Musaylimah, Tulayha and Aswad Ansi, who sought nothing but political power.

In summarising, it should be stressed that Muslims by no means worship Muhammad in any manner, shape or form. All worship is for ALLAH alone, the unseen one true God. There are those who claim that Muhammad established a new religion in His lifetime. Nothing could be further than the truth. Muhammad is not the founder of Islam. The term Mohammedanism is a misconception and highly offensive to Muslims of understanding.

Certainly however, Muslims revere Muhammad as the

Prophet of Islam and Messenger of ALLAH sent to all Mankind till eternity. Both as man and Prophet, Muhammad embodies virtues of patience and tolerance. For Muslims across the globe, He serves as an exemplary role model. His traditions (collections of Hadith) inspire Muslims not to submit to persecution but at the same time not to transgress. They teach Muslims to fight for their rights but in a coordinated manner with force being appropriately directed. Devout Muslims irrespective of nationality strive to lead their lives within the spirit of the Prophet's hadith.

Any misrepresentations concerning the Prophet Muhammad therefore, naturally inflame emotions, particularly among young impressionable Muslims. But such non-constructive propaganda defiling the Prophet Muhammad is often orchestrated in the name of exercising freedom of speech. For some right-wing politicians and intellectuals, Islamaphobia brings for them media attention and fame; in fact for some it is a source of their livelihood and political stratagem. While freedom of speech should challenge our intellect, at the same time it is only fair and proper that caution should be exercised that such freedom does not serve as a source of propagating distorted facts aimed at furthering vested political/commercial interests. For instance, the amateur film 'Innocence of Muslims', produced in the US, which depicted the Prophet Muhammad with ridicule and contempt and portrayed Him as a fraud, womaniser, homosexual and a madman, sparked numerous spontaneous demonstrations in September 2012 against US diplomatic missions across the Muslim world and beyond. These demonstrations reflected the anger and underlying current of resentment of Muslims against what they perceive to be continued attempts by vested Western interests to belittle and discredit the Prophet of Islam.

What caught the attention of the global media and US policymakers were the images of widespread anti-US protests in more than 20 countries, from the Middle East to South-East Asia, as well as North Africa. Regrettably, some of these demonstrations turned violent. The worst violence was the armed attack on the US consulate in Benghazi in Libya which resulted in the death of the US Ambassador to Libya, Chris Stevens, and three other consulate staff. Some media channels covering the events in Benghazi claimed that the US consulate was actually attacked by so-called terrorist cells taking advantage of the situation. There were also less violent protests in the cities of London, Paris, Antwerp and Sydney, though they did result in scuffles with the police with several arrests. Previously, the book 'Satanic Verses' and later the Danish cartoons portraying the Prophet Muhammad as a terrorist had also inflamed emotions across the Muslim World.

While these violent protests have been widely criticised in numerous commentaries as being orchestrated by so-called Muslim extremists, if we strip away the violence emanating from the protests what we are left with is what can be described as a Muslim Awakening similar to that underlying the Arab Spring in 2011. Not only are global Muslims unwilling to endure persecution from their despotic leaders backed by Western governments and large business interests, they are also prepared to reject vested right-wing propaganda belittling the Islamic Faith. While US and Western governments have distanced themselves from such anti-Islamic rhetoric, there is nevertheless a common consensus among the vast sway of Muslims that more can be done by Western governments to tackle such outrageous and bigoted actions by right-wing extremists. What aggravated the crisis over the You Tube video were media reports that the film was produced in the US and allegedly financed by Jewish investors.

Interestingly, we can observe that in September 2012, the Israeli Prime Minister went on record to announce that his government believed Iran was only six months away from developing enriched uranium to fulfil its nuclear military ambition. With Israel finding it increasingly necessary therefore to take a pre-emptive strike against Iran's nuclear facilities to prevent it from developing a nuclear weapon, the anti-US and anti-zionist protests across the Arab world against the You Tube video "Innocence of Muslims" made any Israeli military strike at that time against Iran increasing unlikely, given the fact that the entire region would have erupted into catastrophic uproar if Israel had gone recklessly ahead.

CHAPTER FIVE

Succession and the Seeds of War and Division

So colossal was Muhammad as Man, Prophet and Messenger that upon His death on 12 Rabi'ul-Awwal of the 10th Hijrah (8 June 632 AD) the matter of appointing a Khalifah/Caliph (successor) in terms of providing leadership to the Islamic community became a very real and crucial issue. The Prophet Muhammad left no male heir. The tribal tradition of blood inheritance was consequently ruled out. More importantly, the Holy Qur'an gave no definitive guidance on the question of how a successor was to be chosen after the Prophet Muhammad's death. Neither was there any scope for the Prophet's companions, or anyone else for that matter, to claim leadership as a new prophet, since the Prophet Muhammad was proclaimed by ALLAH as the last Prophet: "Khatam-an-Nabiyyin" (the last of the chain of the true Prophets).

With the Prophet's death the infant Islamic community was in a state of loss and shock, so much so that many in the community found it difficult to come to terms with the reality of the news. In the midst of the confusion and commotion it was the Prophet's closest companion, Chief Counsellor and father-in-law, Abu Bakr, who brought a sense of purpose and direction. While addressing the crowd that had gathered before the Prophet's humble dwelling he declared, "Whosoever worshipped Muhammad, let him know that Muhammad is dead, but whosoever worshipped ALLAH, let him know that ALLAH lives and cannot die."

On the question of who should be the Caliph there was initial disagreement between the Ansar (Muslims of Medina who received and helped the Prophet after his migration from Mecca and were mainly members of the Medinite tribe of Kharaj) and the Muhajirin (followers of the Prophet who migrated from Mecca with, before and after Him to Medina), both claiming that the office should go to one of them. At one stage the Ansars suggested that there should be two Caliphs, one from each of them. In the interests of maintaining solidarity, Umar flatly rejected this proposition. Any such course of action would surely have fragmented the Islamic community. In the course of discussions (which were taking place at the courtyard of Banu Sa'idah) Abu Bakr, at the initiative of Umar, was consequently unanimously elected as the first Caliph of Islam following a public bay'ah at the Mosque the next day. A significant factor behind Abu Bakr's election was the fact that the Prophet Muhammad Himself appointed Abu Bakr to lead the congregational prayers during His last illness. Had any of the Prophet Muhammad's sons survived Him, the issue of succession would surely have taken an entirely different direction, having profound consequences in its aftermath both for the immediate community of Islam and the expansion of Islam into the rest of

Arabia and beyond. Even if Ali had reservations in the election of Abu Bakr as the first Khalifah, Ali's integrity and love for Islam is evidenced by the fact that he did not declare open opposition/hostility to Abu Bakr's Caliphate in the interest of the infant Islamic State.

After his election, Abu Bakr settled the question as to where the Prophet's body should be buried. Recalling the words of the Prophet, *"No prophet dieth but is buried where he died"*, the grave was dug in the floor of Aishah's (the Prophet's widow) room near the couch where the Prophet Muhammad was lying. Consequently, the Prophet Muhammad was buried on the night of 14 Rabi'ul-Awwal in the year of the 10th Hijrah. The Prophet's burial, therefore, took place following the election of Abu Bakr as Caliph.

Centred on the Prophet Muhammad's burial place today sits the Grand palatial compound of the Masjid al-Nabawi. It is revered by Muslims as the second holiest site in Islam after Masjid al-Haram in Mecca, which houses the Ka'bah. Buried alongside the Prophet are two of His closest companions, Abu Bakr and Umar. It is widely accepted by Muslims that a fourth burial place has been set aside for the Prophet Isa (Jesus) who Muslims believe will come at the End of Time to kill the Dajjal (Anti-Christ) and establish ALLAH's rule on Earth. This is discussed further in Chapter Eight.

Abu Bakr along with 'Umar ibn al-Kattab (Umar), 'Uthman ibn Affan of the Umayya clan (Uthman) and the Prophet's cousin and son-in-law, Ali ibn Abu Talib (Ali) are referred to as the righteous/ rightly-guided Caliphs: "Khulafa' Ur Rashidin". They had all heard the revelations from the Prophet himself and been guided by His example. Each served in turn as Caliph. However, with the exception of Abu Bakr, who died from illness, the remaining three Rashidun Caliphs died a violent death, not in war, but as a consequence of conspiracies manifesting themselves in murder and assassinations.

ABU BAKR (632 – 634 AD)

Abu Bakr was indeed a great man. He succeeded in playing a crucial role at a critical time following the announcement of the Prophet's death on Earth. A close trusted friend and confidant of the Prophet, Abu Bakr was also among the first to embrace Islam. He is commonly referred to as al-Siddiq, meaning 'the Truthful'.

Abu Bakr was born into a noble family belonging to the Quraysh tribe of Mecca. A thriving cloth merchant, he was one of Mecca's richest merchants, but following his conversion he dedicated his wealth to the cause of Islam. Many slaves who had embraced Islam and were consequently tortured for doing so, including Bilal, were purchased by Abu Bakr from their masters and given their freedom.

Abu Bakr accompanied the Prophet Muhammad on the flight from Mecca to Medina. He also fought alongside the Prophet on many military campaigns, including the Battle of Badr, the Battle of Uhud and the Battle of the Ditch.

Following Abu Bakr's election as Caliph, his acceptance speech can be said to have laid the foundation of democratic accountability required of leaders in that they are trustees of the people over whom they govern. Abu Bakr is recorded as having said, *"I have been elected your Ameer, although I am not better than you. Help me if I am in the right; set me right if I am in the wrong; obey me as long as I obey ALLAH and His Prophet; when I disobey Him and His Prophet, then obey me not."*

A major achievement of Abu Bakr's brief two-year rule was the victory over the 'false prophets' in what is referred to as the Apostasy Wars. Among these false prophets, Musaylimah proved to be the most dangerous. He claimed that he was also in receipt of a Divine Mission reducing, among other things, the number of compulsory daily prayers, as well as relaxing the duty to fast and the paying of zakat while laying claim to half of Arabia. Misjudging Abu Bakr's political and military prowess, a considerable number of tribes that were hostile to Islam joined ranks with Musaylimah. Initially, the Muslim armies faced defeat. But under the brilliant command of Khalid, the army of Musaylimah was defeated and after fleeing the battlefield he was hunted down and killed.

After the Prophet's death, Abu Bakr realised that the Muslims had to be united under a common enterprise of military expeditions. He launched military campaigns against the Sassanid Empire and Byzantine Empire, setting in motion a trajectory that continued on with Umar and Uthman so that within just a few decades of Muhammad's death the Islamic Empire would become one of the largest in history.

Following the death of numerous Qurra (those who could recite the Qur'anic verses from memory) at the Battle of Yamama against Musaylimah in 632 AD, Abu Bakr, on the insistence of Umar, commenced the task of bringing together all the Divine revelations both written and oral into one volume in what later became the Holy Qur'an. This task he entrusted to Zayd Bin Tabit. It was imperative to do so to prevent the emerging Ummah to facture on religious-political lines.

Sunni Muslims believe that the Divine revelations were written down as one single manuscript and presented to Abu Bakr. The Holy Qur'an was therefore compiled within one year of the death of Prophet Muhammad, when most of His closest Sahabah (companions) were still alive. Prior to his death, Abu Bakr gave this manuscript to Umar and remained with him throughout his rule as the second Righteous Caliph. Prior to his death, Umar gave the manuscript to his daughter Hafsah, who was a widow of the Prophet Muhammad. Uthman's official codex was subsequently prepared from the copy kept with Hafsah.

Securing a political alliance, Abu Bakr was also the Prophet Muhammad's father-in-law. Before his death, Abu Bakr nominated Umar to succeed him as the subsequent Caliph.

UMAR ibn AL-KATTAB (634 – 644 AD)

Umar was not one of the early converts to Islam. In 616 AD, after his initial hostility to Islam and while on a personal mission to kill the Prophet Muhammad, Umar embraced the Faith upon reading verses of the Holy qur'an. So tremendous was his spiritual awakening that Umar would later prove to be one of the staunchest defenders of the Faith. Sunni Muslims revere Umar with the title al-Farooq meaning 'one who distinguishes between right and wrong', believed to have been bestowed by the Prophet Muhammad himself. Born in Mecca into the Banu Adi Clan of the Quraysh Tribe, Umar's father was Khattab ibn Nufayl, who was famed for his intelligence and ruthlessness.

Umar is particularly remembered for his personal attributes. He is known for being tough, bold and a strict disciplinarian. A gifted orator, with his intelligence and overpowering personality he took over his father's mantle as 'arbitrator among tribes'. These personal attributes allowed Umar to become one of Prophet Muhammad's Chief Advisors, and he was also closely associated with Abu Bakr. Like Abu Bakr, Umar too was

Muhammad's father-in-law. The Prophet was married to Umar's daughter, Hafsah. During his rule as the first Righteous Caliph, Abu Bakr relied greatly on Umar and accordingly nominated him to succeed him as the second Caliph.

Following a siege by Muslim Forces that included those of Abu Ubaidah and Khalid, the city of Jerusalem was surrendered by its then Patriarch, Sophronius, to Caliph Umar. Under the terms of the Treaty of Surrender, referred to as the Umari Treaty, no churches were to be razed to the ground while security of life and property were guaranteed. The inhabitants of Jerusalem were captivated by Umar's simple demeanour as he entered the city. Not as a conqueror with pomp and grandeur but a simple clothed rider on camelback with a single aide. This was in stark contrast to the bloody massacre unleashed upon the Muslim and Jewish inhabitants of Jerusalem by the First Crusaders when they took the city in the name of God and Christendom.

Many of the military campaigns undertaken during Caliph Abu Bakr's rule and also briefly during Umar's rule (including conquests of northern Arabia, Syria and parts of Persia) were under the able command of Khalid. His popularity in the Muslim community was rising considerably and Khalid was publicly known as Sayf-ullah, 'Sword of ALLAH'. However, his increasing popularity meant that the Muslim community was attributing military victories to the personality of Khalid. Umar upon becoming Caliph, consequently dismissed him from supreme command of the Muslim Forces in 634 AD on the contention that it is ALLAH that gives victory to the Muslims with Abu Ubaidah being appointed as the new commander-in-chief of the Islamic army. Khalid was later relieved from military service, in 638 AD. In reality there was a potential source of friction between Umar as Caliph and Khalid as Supreme

Commander of the Muslim Forces, or at least their supporters, if Khalid had been allowed to continue in his position.

Umar's rule is credited with a series of lightning conquests, which included victory against the powerful Sassanid Persian Empire, in addition to the conquest of Egypt, Syria and Jerusalem. The Muslim Forces were by now a well-disciplined and successful fighting military machine.

The Persian Military campaign, however, subsequently proved fatal for Umar. With the Persians suffering successive defeats in the Battles of Qadisiya, Chesipon, Jalula and finally in the Battle of Nihavand in 642 AD, the Persian Empire could no longer offer effective resistance (and its King, Yazdgard fled, only to be killed in 651 AD during the rule of Caliph Uthman). The conquest of Persia brought with it many captives who were consequently sold as slaves, including Umar's assassin. His name was Abu Lu'lu', also known as Firoz. While Umar was leading the morning prayers Firoz repeatedly stabbed Umar with a dagger, seriously wounding him. Umar died some days later after succumbing to his injuries in the month of Muharram, 24 Al-Hijri and was buried by the side of the Prophet Muhammad. On his deathbed Umar appointed a six-man committee to elect his successor from amongst themselves rather than himself expressly nominating a successor. The committee members were Uthman ibn Affan; Abd al-Rahman ibn Awf; Ali ibn Abu Talib; Sa'd ibn Abi Waqqas; Zubayr ibn al-Awwam and Talhah ibn Ubayd Allah. (The latter two would subsequently entice Aisha to go into battle with Ali in what has come to be known as the 'Battle of the Camel', for what they perceived as Ali's failure to bring Uthman's assassins to justice quickly enough).

The Committee had asked Ali to become Caliph on the condition that he would follow the Holy Qur'an, Sunnah and

Seerat-e-Sheikhain (the way of the first two Caliphs), to which
Ali replied he would follow the Holy Qur'an and Sunnah. He
argued that if the previous Rashidun Caliphs had followed these,
the subsequent requirement was obsolete. If they had not, then
he had no intention of following their example. Uthman,
however, agreed to accept this condition in its entirety without
question. Some sources claim the Committee elected Uthman
by default, as Ali refused to accept the conditions imposed upon
him, including the condition that he should not proclaim a
Hashemite dynasty. The irony in all this is that following the
assassination of Ali and the subsequent murder of Ali's son
Husayn and his family at Karbala, it was relatives from Uthman's
clan that established the Umayyad dynasty. Unlike the rightly
guided Caliphs, the Rulers of the Umayyad Empire ruled like
kings, enforcing dynastic succession rather than ruling as
Deputies of the Prophet.

UTHMAN ibn AFFAN (644 – 656 AD)

Uthman was born into the wealthy Banu Umayya Clan of the
Quraysh Tribe and belonged to the same clan as Abu Sufyan.
Uthman's father, Affan died while Uthman was still young
positioning him to take up his father's thriving business with a
large inheritance. A nephew of the Prophet Muhammad,
Uthman was also among the first to give his allegiance to Umar
after his election as Caliph.

Uthman's role as Rashidun Caliph is highly controversial, as
there are two competing views put forward by Sunni and Shi'ite
scholars. To begin with, Sunni Islam believes that during
deliberations among the six-man committee set up by Umar to
appoint his successor, Uthman actually favoured Ali as the next

Caliph and Ali favoured Uthman. Shi'ites argue on the other hand that with the exception of Ali and Zubayr, the remaining Committee Members were in fact close relatives of Uthman, and Ali actually protested at the composition of the Committee. It is alleged that the Committee was a deliberate ploy by Umar and Uthman to prevent Ali from being the Caliph. Shi'ite Islam further believes that on the Prophet Muhammad's return to Medina from His last Hajj in 632 AD, Muhammad stopped at a place called Ghadir Khumm (Pond of Khumm) addressing the people there nominating Ali to be His political and spiritual successor. The Sunni branch of Islam denies this.

Uthman's succession as the third Rashidun Caliph had in it the seeds of civil war. His rule was a watershed in the chronicles of the expanding early Islamic State, for unlike his predecessor Umar, Uthman's leadership by comparison was weak for he lacked political maturity sowing the seeds of the fitna (civil war) that ensued.

Sunni Islam, however, views Uthman in a more positive light. Significant military gains and conquests of new territories are attributed to the reign of Uthman, including much of North Africa and Cyprus and the subjugation of Persian Sassanid provinces that rebelled following the death of Umar.

Though Uthman was married to two of Muhammad's daughters at different times, namely Ruqayyah and subsequently after her death Umm Kulthum, which earned Uthman the title of 'Possessor of Two Lights', Shi'ites argue that this did not outrank or supersede Ali's blood ties with Muhammad, as Ali was married to Muhammad's only surviving daughter, Fatimah from Muhammad's first marriage to Khadijah at the time of the Prophet's death. Ali also happened to be the Prophet's first cousin, belonging to the same clan as Muhammad, namely the Banu

Hashim. Furthermore, Hasan and Husayn, the Prophet's beloved grandsons, were Ali's children from his marriage to Fatimah.

The single most important act that signifies Uthman's rule is the transcription of the standardised text of the Holy Qur'an and its subsequent dissemination. The first task he entrusted to Zayd Bin Tabit at the head of a committee which prepared the official codex from the copy kept with Umar's daughter, Hafsah, but in the dialect of the Quraysh. Copies of the official codex were then sent to different provinces of the expanding Islamic State. In doing so Uthman ordered that all unofficial copies of the Holy Qur'an be gathered and destroyed. This opened the door to charges against Uthman of engineering the Holy Qur'an by deliberately omitting Qur'anic verses with explicit references to the virtues of the Prophet's Family, with particular reference to Ali. There is, however, no concrete evidence to substantiate this allegation, as Ali made no attempt to introduce a new standardized copy of the Holy Qur'an when he became Caliph. The Quranic Verses commonly cited as being omitted are those that make up Surah al-Nurayn and Surah al-Wilayah.

The true reason behind the anti-Uthman movement is disputed among Shi'ite and Sunni Muslims. Nevertheless, a common thread emerges from historical texts. To consolidate his power base Uthman installed and retained members of his own tribe to positions of military and political prominence in key Provinces. These included Egypt, Syria, Kufa and Basra. This rapid rise to prominence of men of the Quraysh, who had until the Conquest of Mecca by Muhammad in 630 AD been bitter enemies against Islam, was naturally giving rise to resentment amongst the Muhajirun and Ansars. This Uthman failed to address it by, among other things, retaining Muwaiya, the son of Abu Sufyan, as Governor of Syria.

Discontent among the Muslims in the provinces of the expanding Islamic State was reaching boiling point over the strong rule imposed by the Governors appointed by Uthman. There were grievances over new taxes being introduced to replace war booty, as the pace of conquests had been slowing down since 650 AD. Exploiting increasing tensions between the Hashemite and Umayyad Clans of the Quraysh, a growing movement was emerging to demand the ousting of Uthman as Caliph. In response to the claims of misrule by the Governors of the various Provinces, Uthman did take steps to investigate these allegations. In 654 AD, in an attempt to quell this movement, he called upon his Governors to attend a Council. The following year Uthman called upon those who had any grievance to assemble at Mecca for the annual Hajj, promising to address their legitimate grievances. This provided Uthman with a temporary respite, but the propaganda had by then spread far and wide and the conspiracy against Uthman had become deeply rooted.

The situation in Egypt was becoming increasingly desperate. Similarly, Kufa and Basra were becoming a centre of revolt. In 656 AD contingents of rebels from these Provinces marched on Medina, subsequently besieging Uthman in his house. Uthman shied away from allowing his supporters to engage with the rebels in armed conflict, as he did not want Muslims to shed the blood of other Muslims for the sake of his Caliphate. In a desperate move the rebels later stormed the house, murdering Uthman while, it is understood, he was reciting the Holy Qur'an. Uthman's wife, Naila, tried to shield him from his attackers, but she was wounded herself. This single act of murder sowed the seeds of civil war that would later fragment the Muslim Ummah. Uthman was subsequently buried quietly in fear that the rebels who were still in Medina would desecrate his body.

ALI ibn ABU TALIB (656 – 661 AD)

Ali was the son of Abu Talib, a prominent member of the Tribe of Quraysh belonging to the Hashemite Clan. His father was the Prophet Muhammad's Uncle, making Ali the Prophet's first cousin. Both had a common grandfather, namely Abdul Muttalib. Ali's mother Fatimah bint Asad also belonged to the Hashemite Clan, making him a descendant of Ibrahim's (Abraham's) son Isma'il (Ishmael). A brave warrior, Ali participated in many battles during the time of the Prophet, including the Battles of Badr, Uhud, Khaybar and Hunayn. For his brilliance in battle the Prophet Muhammad conferred on Ali the title of Asadullah, meaning the 'Lion of ALLAH'. Famed for wielding a bifurcated sword, he is also loved and revered by Muslims for his courage, wisdom, knowledge on Islamic Jurisprudence, deep loyalty to Muhammad, equal treatment of all Muslims, compassion and strength of character.

On the eve of Muhammad's flight to Medina, Ali lay under the blanket in Muhammad's bed, thwarting an assassination plot to kill Muhammad. Ali was also among the very first to embrace Islam.

Following the assassination of Uthman a state of confusion and anarchy prevailed in Medina. Rebels to Uthman's rule were still in Medina and looked to Ali to take the reins of the Caliphate. Ali initially refused this offer by the rebels. They then turned to Talhah and Zubayr to accept the role of Caliph, but they also refused this. Faced with an ultimatum by the rebels and on the insistence of prominent companions of the Prophet

Muhammad, Ali subsequently accepted the role of Caliph. Talhah and Zubayr gave their pledge to Ali, along with the people of Medina, though Talhah and Zubayr would later allege that they did so reluctantly.

Soon after becoming the Fourth Rashidin Caliph, in an attempt to consolidate his own position, Ali sought to root out growing Syrian and Persian influence in the Ummah. Going against the advice of learned counsel, Ali ordered that those provincial governors either appointed by or retained by Uthman be dismissed, replacing them with his trusted aides. Most of them were successful in taking charge of the provinces. However, Mu'awiyah, who was kinsman of the slain Uthman, and who was appointed governor of Syria by Umar and retained by Uthman, refused to acknowledge Ali as Caliph and therefore refused to vacate his position as governor. In fact he implicated Ali as an accomplice in Uthman's murder for his neglect in apprehending and punishing Uthman's murderers. As events subsequently panned out it was apparent that Mu'awiyah was only interested in establishing his own dynastic rule and was in no mind to relinquish power. Furthermore, Mu'awiyah had managed to raise a strong army to back his challenge to Ali's Caliphate.

In the meantime, enraged at Ali's inability to bring the murderers of Uthman to justice, Talhah and Zubayr approached Aisha, daughter of Abu Bakr and widow of the Prophet, to rally support against Ali. Aisha, grieving Uthman and angered at the subsequent election of Ali as the new Caliph, also demanded revenge for Uthman's death. Consequently, they succeeded in raising an army. Sensing a challenge to his leadership, Ali too raised an army. The two armies met at Basra in what is known as the Battle of the Camel, marking the beginning of the first Fitna (Civil War) in Islam.

During the course of the battle, fierce fighting took place, resulting in the deaths of many Muslims. Facing defeat, Talhah and Zubayr fled the battlefield and Ali's army took the upper hand. As a mark of victory Ali severed the hamstrings of the camel Aisha was riding on and had her sent back to Medina, after which she withdrew from active frontline political participation. This victory helped to consolidate Ali's rule over the Ummah, with the exception of Syria. Meanwhile, Ali moved his capital to the garrison city which is known as Kufa in present-day Iraq.

To undermine Ali's authority, Mu'awiyah started a propaganda campaign instigating the people to rebel against Ali's Caliphate. Whether it was an oversight on behalf of Ali or not, there was little chance Mu'awiyah was going to relinquish power so readily to a new Governor appointed by Ali, given that Mu'awiyah was in charge of a large battle-hardened army. Furthermore, Mu'awiyah's submission to Ali would surely mean ascendancy of the Hashemite Clan as opposed to the Umayyad Clan in the affairs of the expanding Islamic State. Ali, however, was reluctant to expand on the civil war, as this would lead to the deaths of many Muslims on both sides. Ali therefore opened lines of communication with Mu'awiyah, hoping to gain his allegiance. But this did not yield any results. Consequently, when war became inevitable between Ali and Mu'awiyah both were making preparations for armed engagement.

The two armies met at Siffin near the Euphrates. Despite initial skirmishes, the main battle began in the month of Safar, 37 Al-Hijri. This armed engagement is known as the Battle of Siffin. Within a few days of heavy fighting which resulted in both sides sustaining large casualties, Mu'awiyah's army was on the verge of being routed. In order to avoid a crushing defeat,

Mu'awiyah hatched an ingenious plan by placing copies, as well as pages of the Holy qur'an on the spearheads of his front ranks. This caused confusion and disagreement among different factions of Ali's army and reluctantly he had to recall his forces.

Following cessation of hostilities, it was decided by the warring factions that the matter of the Caliphate should be put to arbitration. While Ali was in favour of arbitration to prevent further bloodshed, to Ali's disappointment however, Abu Musa Ash'ari was chosen to represent him while Amr ibn Aas represented Mu'awiyah. Not everyone in Ali's army was in favour of arbitration, especially when they had been close to victory. Among those who opposed arbitration they later came to be known as Kharijites, meaning 'those who withdrew'. Branding Ali as a traitor for failing to wage jihad against the Umayyad Usurpers, the Kharijites came out of Ali's armed coalition and subsequently rebelled against Ali's rule. In the Battle of Nahrawan which followed, Ali crushed their rebellion with only a handful managing to escape with their lives. But they swore to avenge Ali with his death. (The Kharijites were staunch opponents of Uthman's rule and included many Bedouin tribal leaders, as well as the Prophet's closest friends and relatives who were absolutely determined to uphold the religious traditions that they viewed as conforming to Muhammad's teachings. They are alleged to have been behind the murder of Uthman and the instigators of Ali's election as Caliph who subsequently allied themselves with Ali fighting alongside him at the Battle of the Camel and Siffin.)

The arbitration did not go in favour of Ali and the armed conflict between Ali and Mu'awiyah resumed. Following the fall of Egypt to Mu'awiyah, rebellions against Ali broke out across the Ummah. Taking full advantage of this, Mu'awiyah's armies overpowered those rebellious cities, bringing them under Mu'awiyah's rule. While this was going on Ali was attacked by a Kharijite, ibn Muljam, with a poisonous sword while he was leading the dawn prayer at the site of the present-day Grand Mosque in Kufa. A few days later in the month of Ramadan, 40 Al-Hijri, the last Rashidun Caliph died from his wounds.

There are different opinions over where Ali was buried. Some believe that fearing that his enemies may desecrate his grave, Ali asked his closest friends and relatives to bury him in secret. Most Shi'ites accept that he was buried at the site of the Tomb of Imam Ali in the Imam Ali Mosque in the Iraqi city of Najaf. However another view, usually maintained by some Afghans, notes that Ali's body was taken and buried in the Afghan city of Mazar-e-Sharif at the famous Blue Mosque or Rawze-e-Sharif.

In the immediate aftermath of Ali's death, his son Hasan succeeded his father, but shortly afterwards he capitulated to Mu'awiyah, who had marched an army into Iraq to unseat Hasan's Caliphate. Mu'awiyah in the meantime declared himself Caliph and in doing so founded the Umayyad Dynasty of Caliphs. Subsequently, in the month of Safar, 50 Al-Hijri, Hasan was murdered, poisoned by one of his wives at the instigation of Mu'awiyah, and the Hashemite claim to the Caliphate passed to Husayn, ushering in the second Fitna.

Upon his death in 680 AD, Mu'awiyah appointed his son Yazid I as his heir and successor. Refusing to recognise Yazid I as Caliph, the Shi'ites urged Husayn to claim the Caliphate. In response to their call, Husayn set out for Kufa but was intercepted by the forces of Yazid I at Karbala. Refusing to pay allegiance, Husayn, along with his family and small band of followers, were mercilessly killed in the skirmish that followed, and decapitated. In Husayn's martyrdom Shi'ite Islam found a sense of purpose and direction as a force of rebellion. Even today Shi'ite Muslims across the globe commemorate the events at Karbala, drawing strength and inspiration from the belief that the murder of their third Imam will be redeemed by the awaited twelfth Imam, who they believe to be the Mahdi bringing peace and justice to the world at the end of times.

Shi'ite Islam argues that Ali should have been the immediate successor to the Prophet Muhammad and that he was unfairly denied the Caliphate three times before. They believe that the head of the Muslim Community or Ummah should be a descendant of the Prophet. Shi'ites believe that the Umayyad Caliphs were usurpers of the Caliphate, imposing dynastic succession ruling as kings rather than deputies of the Prophet failing to govern in accordance with the Holy Qur'an and the Prophetic traditions. For the Shi'ites, the Caliph who they term the Imam is also the spiritual representative of the Prophet on earth with the capacity to interpret Divine Law.

The first and second Fitnas (Civil Wars) in Islam threatened to undermine everything the Prophet Muhammad had tirelessly struggled to achieve. After the assassination of Ali, ironically it was descendants of the Prophet's bitterest enemies that ruled the Islamic Ummah, beginning with Mu'awiyah, who was Abu Sufyan's son and had established the Umayyad Dynasty. Critics argue that Uthman was no doubt partly responsible for this and blame should be apportioned to him.

The Prophet Muhammad's vision of a democratic Caliphate was effectively handicapped with the establishment of the Umayyad Dynasty. Dynastic rule is contrary to any notion of a Caliph, who should rather be a representative of the Ummah. This is evidenced by the fact that the Prophet Muhammad did not expressly appoint a named successor despite the fact that the Prophet knew in His heart that He was approaching the end of His life on Earth, as evidenced from the His Farewell Sermon. No doubt the Prophet had done this to avoid any allegation of partiality that might splinter the infant Islamic community after His death. But more importantly, by not appointing a named successor Prophet Muhammad intended to sow the seeds of elected representation. This was centuries before any semblances of democratic values was practised in Europe.

Sunni Scholars argue that Shi'ite Islam is at odds with elective representation. Shi'ites Scholars counter this with the argument that political and religious authority should be vested in those who are most learned on Islamic Jurisprudence. They point to the Sunni despots in the Middle East who live in magnificent splendour, out of touch with the populace over whom they rule, ruthlessly repressing demands for political pluralism.

Islam requires Muslim rulers not to be tyrannical. They are on a par with the people they govern. It is the duty of every Muslim to overthrow tyrannical despots, for they rule not in the way of Islam. At the very core of political Islam lies elected representation. The Middle East is infested with predominantly Sunni despots who purport to rule in name of Islam yet have deviated from the principles set out by the Prophet Muhammad. If we take the example of the Rashidun Caliphs, they did not separate themselves from the populace by living in luxury and grandeur. In fact, it is well documented that all the Rashidun Caliphs led ordinary lives and were accessible by the people they governed. They all worked tirelessly to uplift the poor and the destitute. Abu Bakr in his acceptance speech went so far as to give permission to the Ummah to remove him should he fail to rule in the way of the Holy Qur'an and the Prophet's Sunnah.

The Arab Spring that began in 2011 was a reaction to decades of despotic rule. It ignited in Tunisia, quickly engulfing North Africa and the Middle East. Despite stiff resistance by entrenched dictators and their military establishment, the struggle of the Muslim Ummah continues to reassert itself in the way of true Islam. It would be premature to conclude that the Arab Spring is effectively dead in light of the military coup against a democratically elected President in Egypt and the brutal repression being carried out by the Syrian and Bahraini Regimes on its peoples. The Arab Revolt is currently experiencing a watershed. What it needs is a renewed revival of the inspiration that sparked the uprising.

Though the Arab Spring will be discussed in more detail in later chapters, it is important to note here that it is imperative that the Islamic Awakening is not hijacked by both the political and military 'Old Guard' lying in wait on the sidelines.

CHAPTER SIX

Contemporary Islam and the Rise of Militancy

Western foreign policy has actively provoked an extremist response from a passionate enemy unable to channel its frustration into constructive opposition; instead it has found an outlet to express its anguish in the form of terrorism. Without condoning terrorism in any manner, shape or form, let us examine this observation, as many in the Muslim World believe that their grievance is not without reason or foundation.

At the very heart of the resentment lies the animosity between Israel and the Palestinians. Much of the anger results from the continued growth of illegal Israeli settlements on occupied Palestinian territory, Israel's disproportionate use of force against Palestinian protesters, the stranglehold siege of Gaza, reports of torture of Palestinian detainees being held without charge or trial, and the unrelenting support of successive US Administrations in favour of Israel with no clear sign of a sustainable Peace Process in the offing. Anguish also lies over the status of the Old City of Jerusalem, for it is a city sacred to Muslims across the globe, because it contains the Noble Sanctuary (Haram Al-Sharif mountain) encompassing the Dome of the Rock (that houses the foundation/ascension stone) and the Al-Aqsa Mosque (Al-masjid Al-aqsa), which marks the third holiest site in Islam. Muslims firmly believe the ascension stone marks the place from where the Prophet Muhammad ascended to Heaven on "The Night Journey" commonly referred to as the Mi'raj. For many US Presidents and their Administrations, trying to effect a peace deal between the two belligerents is often only a foreign policy box-ticking exercise resulting in no meaningful outcome, for they crave the financial and voting support of Zionist organizations, their allies and the Jewish lobby. Former US President Harry S. Truman once remarked that the whole Palestinian issue could be resolved if US politics were kept out of the equation, and this is as true today as it was then.

The blockade of the Gaza Strip by Israel was triggered by the capture of Gaza by Hamas in June 2007 following violent clashes with rival Palestinian faction Fatah after President Mahmoud Abbas dismissed the Hamas-led government, declaring a state of emergency. The blockade has resulted in appalling living conditions for its 1.5 million inhabitants, with sanctions sucking the life out of Gaza and forcing its inhabitants to rely on a network of underground tunnels for supplies. The blockade has however galvanized support for their plight both within and beyond the Muslim world. Israel, however, has always argued that the blockade is essential to prevent Hamas from obtaining weapons and to limit Hamas rocket attacks from the Gaza Strip on its cities.

Despite this, under international pressure to lift the blockade following the deadly 'Gaza freedom flotilla' raid, Israel started easing restrictions back in June 2010, allowing only strictly civilian goods to enter Gaza. Nevertheless, assessments carried out in January and February 2011 by the United Nations Office for the Coordination of Humanitarian Affairs (UNOCHA) of the effects of the measures to ease the access restrictions concluded that they did not result in a significant improvement in people's living conditions. In June 2012 it reported that 44% of Gazans were food insecure and 80% aid recipients, with 35% of Gaza's farmlands and 85% of its fishing waters being totally or partially inaccessible due to Israeli-imposed restrictions.

All too often we hear of civilian deaths resulting from frequent Israeli airstrikes against what Israeli Defence Forces (IDF) term 'terror activity sites' responsible for firing rockets at Israel. This results in cries for revenge against Israel by Hamas that often take the form of rocket attacks, so there appears no end to this vicious cycle of killings.

In May 2011 the United States President, Barack Obama, made official the long-held but rarely stated US support for a future Palestinian state based on borders and lines that existed before the 1967 Middle East war alongside mutually agreed (negotiated) land swaps. The President nonetheless reiterated the United States commitment to Israel's security as "unshakable" and said "every state has the right to self-defence, and Israel must be able to defend itself - by itself – against any threat." The Israeli reaction to the pre-1967 border proposition was naturally predictable, coming in its usual uncompromising stubborn rhetoric. The Prime Minister of Israel, Benjamin Netanyahu, claimed that the 1967 lines were key to Israel's security. The Prime Minister also refused to work with any Palestinian Government that would include Hamas in the negotiations, calling them the "Palestinian version of al-Qaeda". But surely, the way forward to securing a credible and sustainable peace cannot be realized by making unrealistic demands prior to starting negotiations. Hamas too needs to lower the ratchet on its anti-Israeli rhetoric.

The President of the Palestinian Authority, Mahmoud Abbas, undertook efforts in September 2011 following an impasse in negotiations with Israel over its settlement building activities in the West Bank and East Jerusalem to secure a vote at the United Nations on Palestinian statehood. A successful application for full membership in the United Nations, however, requires a recommendation from the United Nations Security Council and a two-thirds majority in the United Nations General Assembly. As a permanent member of the Security Council, the United States had made it abundantly clear that it would veto any such recommendation for United Nations membership, while Britain and France remained undeclared. The US went as far as threatening to withdraw United Nations funding if the bid on Palestinian statehood became successful. Interestingly, United States law bars funding by the US to any United Nations Body that grants full membership to Palestine before a peace agreement between Israel and Palestine is reached. Accordingly, in October 2011, when the United Nations Educational, Scientific and Cultural Organisation (UNESCO) voted to recognize Palestine as a full member, the US withdrew around $60 million in financial support to it. It must be emphasized here that UNESCO membership has no formal bearing on any bid for Palestinian statehood.

The Obama administration argued that Palestinian statehood without a negotiated peace agreement with Israel would isolate Israel internationally and deal a major setback to Israeli-Palestinian peace prospects. Mr Abbas however stressed that it was necessary for Palestinians to assert the legitimacy of their claim to territory under pressure from Israeli settlements and that they had no choice but to believe that negotiations had run their course. Consequently, the bid for United Nations membership was a logical conclusion to the stalemate. The US insisted, however, that Hamas denounce its use of terror and accepts Israel's right to exist.

In the end, despite the threat of a US veto, Mr Abbas submitted a letter requesting UN membership for Palestine to UN Secretary-General Ban Ki-moon. The Secretary-General handed the request over to the UN Security Council, which in turn placed the application before its Committee on the Admission of New Members for their recommendation. The Committee, however, was unable to make a unanimous recommendation back to the Security Council with respect to the request for Palestinian Membership in the United Nations, so the Palestinian bid fell short of the nine 'yes' votes necessary for the resolution to pass the UN Security Council. The US was, as a result, spared from using its power of veto, which would have run the risk of alienating the Muslim world on a crucial policy decision that would have opened itself up to criticisms of hypocrisy and double standards by opposing the self-determination of Palestinians, yet supporting uprisings in Libya, Egypt and Syria.

The fact remains that the US was and still is prepared and willing to exercise its power of veto on the issue of Palestinian statehood. So much so that when again in late November 2012, Mahmood Abbas returned to the UN, this time to upgrade Palestinian membership from an 'observer' to a 'non-member state', the US exercised its veto, this time at the General Assembly of the UN. Among the 193 member states of the General

Assembly, 138 voted in favour and 9 against with 41 abstentions, including the United Kingdom and Germany. Nevertheless, it was enough, and Palestine now enjoys the same status at the UN as the Vatican. More crucially it will be able to gain access to the International Criminal Court (ICC), not only to pursue claims of war crimes against Israel but also for Israel's ongoing settlement building on occupied territory. Should Palestine choose to do this, Israel and the US will no doubt retaliate, with crippling financial implications. Prime Minister Benjamin Netanyahu of Israel both naturally and predictably dismissed the General Assembly vote, calling it "meaningless", and claimed it "won't change anything on the ground." He must have meant it, for within days of the vote the Israeli government announced that it would go ahead with building new settlements.

The continued building of Israeli settlements with impunity on occupied Palestinian territories is a source of much resentment by Palestinians and is proving to be a major obstacle to peace efforts. This is indicative of the latest round of US-sponsored peace talks, which began in July 2013 under the stewardship of US Secretary of State John Kerry and resulted in the tendering of resignations by the Palestinian peace delegation in November 2013, blaming Israel for sabotaging the peace talks by approving the construction of new settlements on occupied territories (West Bank and annexed East Jerusalem). It may be worth noting that Article 49 of the Fourth Geneva Convention provides that an occupying power is forbidden from transferring part of its own civilian population into the territory it occupies. United Nations Security Council resolution 446, adopted on 22 March 1979, concerning the issue of Israeli settlements in the "Arab territories occupied by Israel since 1967, including Jerusalem", determined "that the policy and practices of Israel in establishing settlements in the Palestinian and other Arab territories occupied since 1967 have no legal validity and constitute a serious obstruction to achieving a comprehensive, just and lasting peace in the Middle East". The Resolution was adopted by 12 votes to none with 3 abstentions, from Norway, the United Kingdom and the United States of America.

The International Court of Justice considers these settlements in the occupied territories as illegal too, as do some Western powers. Yet Israel continues to expand existing settlements, in addition to settling new areas in the form of settlement outposts. Successive Israeli Governments have always emphasized that all settlements are legal and consistent with international law.

Despite the settlements' illegality, ironically Israeli firms operating in these illegal settlements continue to engage in international trade, mainly in fresh fruits and vegetables, with considerable exports to Europe securing substantial revenues. Though Israel and the EU have trade agreements, surely this cannot be intended to benefit goods produced on illegal settlements in the occupied territories? Furthermore, EU firms, including British businesses, have extensive commercial involvement in illegal Israeli settlements, particularly in construction.

It is understandable why the US and particularly Israel are apprehensive of a unilateral declaration and subsequent recognition by International Bodies of Palestinian statehood, as this would threaten both US and Israeli interests. It would undermine accepted frameworks for peace based on negotiated agreements in which the US no doubt wishes to see itself as a major player. Understandably perhaps, many Muslims across the Muslim World perceive the unrelenting support in favour of

Israel by Western Powers, in particular the US, as not only injustice to the plight of Palestinians but by extension an underlying antipathy to Islam and Muslims which feeds substance to the rhetoric that the 'West is at war with Islam'. The amendment adopted at the US Democratic National Convention in September 2012 referencing Jerusalem as the capital of Israel, as well as Republican Presidential Candidate Mitt Romney's public support of Jerusalem as Israel's Capital in the run-up to the 2012 Presidential Election, illustrates the tight grip Jewish donors and pro-Israeli lobby groups have over US party politics.

Ironically, despotic regimes in the Middle East express their support for the oppressed Palestinian people while enforcing an iron grip on their own populations, denying them their civil liberties. In this regard, power politics is surely the art of the possible. And yet when Israeli airstrikes pounded Gaza in November 2012 in response to rockets fired by Hamas into Israeli cities, those despotic regimes could only muster calls demanding an end to the bloodshed.

It was Egypt's then new democratic government that seized the initiative to broker a ceasefire between Hamas and Israel that came into effect on 21 November 2012. The preceding eight days of airstrikes and rocket attacks left more than 150 Palestinians and five Israelis dead, mostly civilians. Hamas claimed victory over the ceasefire, claiming that Israel had indirectly recognized Hamas on a political level when up until then Israel had branded Hamas a terrorist organization. The Egyptian President's credibility in brokering the ceasefire later proved to be a pretext for Mohamed Morsi to grant himself sweeping new powers in the name of safeguarding national security, which he subsequently had to relinquish following the clashes between pro and anti-Muslim Brotherhood activists that rocked Cairo in December 2012. Following months of political stalemate and a failing economy the Egyptian military finally ousted Mohamed Morsi from power on 3 July 2013, suspending the constitution in what can only be described as a military coup against Egypt's first democratically-elected President.

Let us turn our attention to the Arab Spring and the contemporary relationship between the West and the Muslim Ummah. Some political scientists have commented that the Arab Spring is a direct consequence of the 2003 invasion and occupation of Iraq. Such an observation is too simplistic in light of events as they continue to unfold. Rather, we should be critically assessing whether the dominance of Sunni Islam in the Middle East is under threat from Shi'ite Islam in light of the Arab Spring, or as the Iranians prefer to call it, the 'Islamic Awakening'. When the ruling (Sunni) Al-Khalifa family of Bahrain called on the support of Saudi troops in March 2011, albeit under the aegis of 'GCC forces' (a six-nation regional coalition of Sunni ruled countries) to assist in what can appropriately described as a brutal crackdown on the (predominantly Shi'ite) peoples' uprising against its rule, the Western Powers took a relatively cautious approach, not only in terms of their public criticism of the crackdown but the lack of comprehensive Western media coverage of the murders, arrests and disappearances of pro-democracy protesters. The US Fifth Fleet, based in Bahrain, is critical to US political and military interests in the region, in particular to checking any ambitious military moves on the part of Shi'ite-dominated Iran. Along with Iraq, Bahrain has a sizable Shi'ite population. If we look at the demography of the Middle East, Shi'ites represents a significant percentage of the population in several states.

According to the Pew Forum Report of 2009 on global Muslim populations, the percentage of the Muslim population that is Shi'ite in Bahrain is between 65-75%; in Iraq between 65-70%; in Lebanon between 45-55% and in Yemen between 35-45%. The nightmare scenario for the West, and in particular Israel, is whether the Arab Spring will usher in democratically-elected Shi'ite governments across the Middle East, backed by Iran with potential nuclear weapons. That would almost certainly change the political dynamics in the region. Surviving Sunni despots will inevitably embark upon frantic purchasing of conventional weapons to repress any opposition to their rule, be it from an internal or an external source. It may also lead to nuclear arms proliferation in the region. Arguably this would leave Israel particularly vulnerable in a volatile landscape.

What the Arab Spring has done is to galvanise a whole generation of Muslims in the region. Starting with Tunisia, on 17 December 2010, in a single act of defiance by Mohamed Bouazizi by setting himself on fire in protest against the corruption and harassment of government officials, the anger and frustration felt by young Tunisians against autocratic rule and failing economic circumstances subsequently spread across North Africa and the Middle East like wildfire. Sceptics, however, perceive selective Western support for freedom and democracy in the Middle East and Northern Africa as nothing more than securing their military and economic interests. In fact, post 9/11, it is widely perceived that the oil-rich countries of North Africa and the Middle East are experiencing a new wave of imperialism and empire building by Western powers, who are eager to secure energy supplies as well as establishing their military and political hegemony in that region.

In March 2011, Western Powers intervened militarily in

Libya with Britain, France and the US taking a leading role to prevent what they believed was a potential massacre of civilians by Colonel Gaddafi's autocratic regime in the Libyan city of Benghazi. Strangely enough, up until then, the West, in particular Britain, France and Spain, had found it acceptable to do business with Gaddafi. Swiftly pushing through UN Security Council Resolution 1973 adopted under Chapter VII of the UN Charter, the Resolution formed the basis for military intervention in the Libyan civil war. It demanded an immediate ceasefire and authorised the international community to establish a no-fly zone and to use 'all means necessary' short of foreign occupation to protect civilians. This consequently took the form of airstrikes under NATO command and the arming of anti-Gaddafi forces, which resulted in the capture and summary execution of Colonel Gaddafi on 20 October 2011, allegedly by National Transition Council (NTC) fighters in his hometown of Sirte, east of the capital Tripoli, after his convoy was attacked by NATO warplanes.

In terms of the financial costs of waging this military campaign, it was no doubt a substantial burden on the taxpayers of the lead participating countries. It is reported that the United Kingdom spent $333 million and France $813 million, with the US spending $1.3 billion. But more importantly and ironically, the number of civilian casualties was regrettably high, despite the fact that the legal basis of UN Security Council Resolution 1973 was to protect civilian life. According to the NTC, 30,000 people were killed up until September 2011. All sides to the conflict have inflicted civilian deaths. They include government, rebel and coalition forces. Furthermore, Human Rights Watch called on NATO to investigate the numerous civilian deaths resulting from its air strikes, despite the fact that NATO claimed that it did everything possible to minimise risk to civilians.

From the start of the campaign there were allegations that the limits imposed by UN Resolution 1973 and by US law were being violated. At the end of May 2011, Western troops were captured on film by Al-Jazeera in Libya, despite Resolution 1973 specifically prohibiting 'a foreign occupation force of any form on any part of Libyan territory'. The news report did however state that armed Westerners and not Western troops were on the ground. What it boils down to is the semantics of the language used by the media and in UN Security Council Resolutions.

Critics of the military campaign allege that the real impetus behind the intervention was regime change, as well as gaining control of Libya's substantial oil reserves and financial capital. As a member of OPEC, Libya was a major oil producer prior to the uprising. In addition, Libya is alleged to have had substantial gold reserves in its Central Bank. Meanwhile, with the fall of Colonel Gaddafi, lucrative deals have been signed with Western corporate bodies to develop the infrastructure which was destroyed in the civil war. The General National Forces Alliance (NFA) which was elected by popular vote in July 2012 took over from the NTC as Libya's legislative authority, picking up 39 of the 80 seats in the General National Assembly reserved for political parties. Its real test came in August 2012 when the US Ambassador to Libya and three other consulate staff were killed, allegedly by armed groups taking advantage of the rage that followed airing of the controversial video 'The innocence of Muslims'. The NFA surely has its task cut out in disarming the many Libyans who acquired arms during the uprising against the former dictator Colonel Gaddafi. In fact, it is reported that the influx of weapons during the course of the 'Libyan Campaign' has helped to consolidate the position of extremist elements operating in the 'Islamic Maghreb'.

Before proceeding any further, let us briefly examine some of the perceived historical root causes of mistrust between Muslims and the West. The commercial expansion of Europe in the 17th century brought about by the industrial revolution saw European powers competing with one another to secure monopolies over the supply of spices, tea, silk and other lucrative trade commodities from Asia, Southeast Asia and Africa to Europe. Consequently, over the next few centuries Islamic lands bore the brunt of European colonization. With victory at the Battle of Plassey in 1757, the East India Company under Robert Clive secured a permanent foothold in Bengal, following which the British Empire was ruling over the entire Indian subcontinent by the 1850s. In 1830 France occupied Algeria, taking Tunisia in 1881. In 1839 the British occupied Aden, and Egypt followed in 1882. Sudan was occupied in 1899. In 1912 the Italians occupied Libya, while the French were in control of Morocco. Following the defeat of the Central Powers in the First World War that included the Ottoman Empire, which capitulated on 30 October 1918; it was subsequently divided up among the victorious Allies, drawing the boundaries of the modern Middle East. The League of Nations granted France a mandate to control both Syria and Lebanon, while the British were given Iraq, Transjordan and Palestine. As for Muslim-populated lands in Central Asia, these were absorbed into the USSR.

The claim that Western colonial powers brought civilization in the form of culture and enlightenment to their Muslim colonies is grossly ill informed and exaggerated. Prior to European colonization, throughout the European Middle Ages, Islamic lands were the hub of innovation and creativity, particularly in the sciences, philosophy and architecture. Magnificent cities such as Cordoba dotted the lands of the Caliphate.

In the years following the end of the Second World War most of the Muslim colonies, including those in Arabia and Northern Africa, gained independence from their colonial masters. Many of these struggles for independence transformed the political mindset of the Muslim World, putting their complete trust in nationalism and secularism.

With China and India emerging as economic super-powers and likely to command more than one-half of the world's population by 2050, thereby making them the largest global consumer market with a thirst for energy and natural resources which will surpass the likes of Europe and the United States, the West has every reason to be worried. With current trends, China and India will also be the largest manufacturers of consumer products, with a vast employable workforce surpassing the entire populations of Europe and the US. To add to this, the US has a multi-trillion dollar debt. According to the US Treasury Department, as of November 2013, 1.317 trillion dollars is owned by China making it the largest foreign holder of U.S. debt after Japan. While the 'U.S. Dollar' is currently the standard currency for most international trade, including crude oil, theoretically speaking such commercial transactions can be carried out in whatever currency the parties involved decides. Should major oil-producing countries therefore conduct transactions other than in US Dollars this would have a catastrophic effect on the clout of the 'US Petrodollar' and the United States money markets. This may very well be the future consequence of the continuing shift of global economic growth eastwards towards China and India. In fact, the Chinese yuan (RMB) may potentially replace the dominance of the US dollar in terms of global trade.

If we look at the second global currency, the Euro, with the

Eurozone facing increasing uncertainty over bailouts for EU member states, as we saw particularly with Greece in 2012, this has definitely played into the hands of US fortunes, with the US dollar increasingly looking like remaining the currency of choice for the time being.

No doubt the currency of global trade will continue to dominate world finance and US global influence. Indeed, the US may also be seeking to counterbalance increasing Chinese clout by fostering trade and cooperation with Southeast Asian countries which benefit from skilled cheap labour. This is illustrated by the choice of countries President Obama first visited after his re-election in November 2012. They included Myanmar, Thailand and Cambodia.

With the West facing economic implosion unless it can pull itself out of its current financial meltdown, trade will always take precedence over human rights issues. We have seen this with the West in their dealings with Saudi Arabia, China and now Myanmar. Myanmar has recently witnessed serious sectarian violence in its northern Rakhine State between Buddhist Rakhinis and minority Muslim Rohingyas, with UK-based NGOs reporting that both the Burmese army and police were also targeting Muslim Rohingyas through mass arrests, violence, rape and systematic discrimination since a state of emergency was declared there on 10 June 2012. Serious questions need to be answered by the Mayanmar authorities as to whether the massacre of Muslim minorities is indeed state sponsored. The loss of life, destruction of property, the displacement of families from their homesteads and the inaction of the Government and local administration in affected areas in terms of reparations and resettlement have been appalling. The ethnic cleansing must stop! For an impoverished country that is only recently beginning to assert itself on the global stage as an up-and-coming democracy after decades of military oppression, it is unfortunate.

Consequently, the crucial issue for the Muslim Ummah is how the Western powers go about addressing their concerns now in preparation for the future, especially when they are facing what appears to be a protracted economic recession following the financial turmoil that came about in 2008 following the credit crunch bank bailouts. Right-wing political elements are likely to argue that slow economic growth and the potential of a triple-dip recession in the United States and some European countries, coupled with the Eurozone crisis, leaves little room for complacency on the part of Western political leaders. But surely the emphasis should be on cooperation with a democratic Muslim leadership and not confrontation. Indeed, interesting times lie ahead.

A protracted armed confrontation between Iran and Western powers over Iran's alleged nuclear programme to develop a nuclear bomb will not only destabilize the Middle East, which is very much already a powder keg, but will predictably send fuel prices rocketing, creating anarchy in the commodities markets. It is extremely likely that the Straits of Hormuz will be transformed into a naval war zone, threatening the supply of a third of global oil supplies. Ultimately, it will be the consumers in the West who will have to bear the brunt of the financial catastrophe that will follow any new protracted military engagement in that region. Consequently, no doubt this will have political overtones in Western domestic politics.

The Western powers will also have to make contingency plans to enter into agreements with the likes of for example, Venezuela, Nigeria and Russia to meet any downturn in oil supplies, unless of course they are confident that they will be able to invade and install a pro-Western government in Iran in very much the same way as they have done in Iraq and Afghanistan, or aid an armed insurgency as they did in Libya. There is substance in the argument that if Iran does attain a nuclear weapon this will usher in a nuclear arms race in the Middle East, but only because Sunni despots will have everything to fear for from a Shi'ite nuclear military power in their midst.

There are also potentially serious implications for Israel's security in the region, given the political rhetoric that often comes out of Iran. At the same time, it is argued that if Iran does eventually succeed in making a nuclear bomb, this would bring in a nuclear deterrent in the Middle East. In any case, any military adventure on the part of Israel in the direction of Iran is likely to have dangerous repercussions in the Middle East. Even a surprise military airstrike on Iranian nuclear facilities by Israeli warplanes is very likely to galvanise hatred by Muslims against Israel and her allies in the region and beyond. This will only provide extremist groups with the notion of 'just cause' to recruit new members to carry out acts of criminality against Israeli and Western interests.

With the election of Cleric Hassan Rouhani in June 2013 as the new Iranian President, it will be interesting to see how he deals with the West with respect to Iran's nuclear enrichment programme. Under Iran's former President Mohammad Khatami, Mr Rouhani served as chief nuclear negotiator; during his period of office no major economic sanctions were imposed on Iran, as it was viewed then as being cooperative with inspectors of the International Atomic Energy Agency (IAEA). Having won just over 50% of the vote, Mr Rouhani has for now the populist support to fend off any internal dissent if he wishes to pursue reformist policies. Widely reported as being a moderate, he surely has the difficult task of promoting Iran's economic interests for the benefit of its citizens.

Iran must find a way to overcome its present political isolation and economic sanctions imposed by the West without compromising its sovereignty. Mr Rouhani must tackle hardliners from within Iran's political establishment. Iran's political power structure is far from transparent.

Without a doubt, Israel will be observing the political vibes within Iran, particularly following the diplomatic initiative taken by Mr Rouhani at the 2013 UN General Assembly Meeting to bring a solution to the 'nuclear issue'. Following on from that UN meeting, Iran and the five permanent members of the UN Security Council, along with Germany (P5 plus 1) met in Geneva in November 2013 to work at achieving a working framework on 'rolling back' Iran's nuclear ambition while at the same time easing sanctions. All sides hailed the outcome of the talks as a 'first step'. Prior to the next round of negotiations, in the interim six-month period Iran will stop enriching uranium to weapons grade (20% purity and above). Any existing stockpiles will be converted to harmless oxide. Nor will Iran increase its store of uranium processed to the 5% level needed for nuclear power stations. Iran will also not fuel its plutonium reactor in Arak, while it will allow IAEA inspectors access to its nuclear power plants. In return P5 plus 1 will ease sanctions to the tune of 7 billion US dollars and will not impose any new nuclear-related sanctions in the interim six months.

It is indeed in everyone's interests to come to a long-term agreement. For Iran it is increasingly important, as its ever-growing youth population seek to reap the financial benefits of the global economy, otherwise the Iranian political establishment is likely to face a domestic backlash. Israel is indeed sceptical of any compromise between Iran and the West, particularly with the US. To appease Israeli stakeholders and players within the US political structure, the US government has repeatedly emphasised that it would impose new sanctions in the event of a breach, warning European businesses not to rush in to strike any substantial business deals with Iran prior to any comprehensive agreement being reached.

The West is often accused of providing political and military support to oppressive regimes in North Africa and the Middle East in exchange for economic benefits (oil rights), often exchanging intelligence resulting in the torture of so-called terrorists. Post 9/11 this form of torture had reportedly taken the form of enhanced interrogation techniques such as water boarding, sleep deprivation and subjecting the prisoner to prolonged stress positions, amongst others. The plight of Abdel Hakim Belhadj, who played a leading role in the fall of former Libyan dictator Colonel Gaddafi and who attempted to sue MI6 over his alleged rendition by the CIA in 2004, is a stark example. In December 2013, a High Court Judge struck out Mr Belhadj's case on the grounds that if it were allowed to proceed it could damage British national interests. In fact, the basis of Mr Justice Simon's decision was that it was not within his jurisdiction to decide whether "the conduct of US officials acting outside the US was unlawful in circumstances where there are no clear and incontrovertible standards for doing so and where there is incontestable evidence that such an inquiry would be damaging to the national interest". (It would have been interesting, nevertheless, to have observed the outcome of Mr Belhadj's case, even if it had been heard under the recently enacted controversial Justice and Security Act 2013, which allows for trials to be held in secret where they involve intelligence and secret documents. Civil liberties groups/lawyers have, however, criticized this legislation as a curb on individual civil rights.)

The United States and Europe continue to provide political and military assistance to the non-democratic despotic regimes of Bahrain and Saudi Arabia. For the West, the Saudi regime will be a key ally should they decide to impose further crippling economic sanctions on Iran. At the same stroke the US needs the pro-US Bahraini Regime if military incursions with Iran become inevitable, as their Navy's Fifth Fleet is currently based in Bahrain.

It should be emphasized that despots are only as powerful as their generals make them out to be. That is why in those countries where the people have taken to the streets to protest against despotic rule in favour of political pluralism, including Tunisia, Egypt, Libya, Yemen, Bahrain and Syria, the security forces have clamped down on protesters with deadly force. The fall of a dictator even by popular revolution will therefore make very little difference unless the army steps aside from political interference. In December 2011 scores of Egyptian protesters were killed or brutally beaten in sporadic clashes with Egyptian security forces for demanding a transition to civilian rule by Egypt's interim military leadership following the fall of Hosni Mubarak earlier in February 2011 (after an 18-day long uprising removed him from power). Cairo's iconic Tahrir Square was again the focal point for protest.

The Supreme Council of the Armed Forces (Scaf) appeared in no mood to hand over power to a civilian government at the time without first securing concessions and guarantees for themselves in any future political power structure for Egypt.

They played the Western Powers with their assurances that the Peace Treaty with Israel was secure with them. The West will surely demand similar assurances of peace from new regimes that have emerged or are likely to emerge as a consequence of the Arab Spring. Consequently, upon being narrowly elected with 51% of the vote in the second round of the 2012 Presidential Elections, the new Egyptian President, Mohamed Morsi of the Muslim Brotherhood, stated that he would honour Egypt's Peace Treaty with Israel. Abrogation of the 1979 Camp David Accords by Egypt would effectively put Egypt in a state of war with Israel. This is something that even the Muslim Brotherhood seeks to avoid. Interestingly enough, Mr Morsi's election victory was achieved despite the fact that the Egyptian Parliament was dissolved only days before by Egypt's Supreme Constitutional Court on the pretext that the parliamentary elections – won by the Muslim Brotherhood-led Democratic Alliance - were null and void. It may be worth noting that Mohamed Morsi's rival, Ahmed Shafi, who was an ex-general and former Prime Minister under disposed President Mubarak, secured 48% of the vote. Had the Supreme Council of the Armed Forces got their way with Ahmed Shafi winning the presidential elections, widespread violence would certainly have gripped Egypt back then.

Mohamed Morsi's presidency was undermined by the military, who were reluctant to hand over total effective power to a civilian government without concessions. In an act of defiance against the military, Mr Morsi, soon after taking power as President, issued a decree recalling Parliament. After a brief session, the Supreme Constitutional Court overturned President Morsi's decree to recall parliament on 10 July 2012. Mr Morsi agreed not to escalate the situation and to respect the Supreme Court's decision. A subtle power struggle ensued and a new constitution was drafted and subsequently ratified by a referendum in December 2012. In February 2013, President Morsi announced that Parliamentary elections would be held in April of the same year. But that seemed doubtful in light of court rulings on the electoral law and threats of boycott.

Undermining the democratic process, Mr Morsi was effectively forcibly ousted from power on 3 July 2013 by the Egyptian Armed Forces after it had earlier issued an ultimatum to the President in light of large scale anti-government demonstrations across Egypt that centred on Cairo. As part of the coup strategy the military suspended the constitution, appointing Adil Mansoor, the head of the Supreme Constitutional Court, as interim head of state, to be assisted by an interim council until new presidential and parliamentary elections were held. Many media outlets were raided and closed while senior Muslim Brotherhood leaders were arbitrarily arrested, no doubt with the intention of avoiding an organised backlash by pro-Morsi supporters. The Egyptian Army had again proved that despite the downfall of Hosni Mubarak in February 2011 following widely-supported nationwide mass demonstrations, it was still the main power broker in Egypt and was willing and able to step into the political arena. Ironically, the 2013 military coup was supported by celebrations across Egypt. For them, Mr Morsi failed to meet their expectations, particularly in reviving the economy and ensuring public security, among other concerns. Moreover, Mr Morsi was viewed with contempt, by secular forces in particular, for his pro-Islamic stance, which was viewed as a credible threat to their secular principles. Mr Morsi's increasing authoritarian style of leadership was also being seen at odds with democratic principles.

However, grave concern centres on the violent and bloody clampdown by the military on pro-Morsi supporters. Hundreds of people are reported to have been shot dead, with many more being wounded in bloody clashes between protesters loyal to ousted President Mohammed Morsi and security forces. Among the bloodiest clashes, at least 82 protesters were reportedly killed on 27 July 2013 near the Raba'a Al Adiwiya Mosque. Then again on 14 August 2013 hundreds were reportedly killed during a drive to clear protesters' camps, provoking international condemnation but no real sanctions against a repressive military regime.

The Military had declared that elections would be held in 2014 following a referendum on a new charter to replace the so-called 'Islamist constitution' passed during Mr Morsi's presidency. This constitutional referendum took place on 14 and 15 January 2014, with 98% of those who turned out to vote backing a new draft constitution. The turnout was 38.6% of the 54 million eligible voters. Under the new draft constitution political parties are prevented from being formed on the basis of religion while at the same time it empowers the military to appoint the Defence Minister for the next eight years. An uncertain and potentially dangerous period lies ahead, especially with General Abdul-Fattah al-Sisi, former head of the Egyptian military that effectively disposed of Mr Morsi, winning the presidential election's held between 26 and 28 May 2014 with the Muslim Brotherhood being branded a 'terrorist organisation'. In light of figures announced by the Presidential Election Commission, interestingly the election was marked by a relatively low turnout (47.4% of the 54 million eligible voters), of which Mr Sisi won 96.9% of the votes cast. In fact, the vote was extended to three days because of the initial low turnout, backed by a threat of a fine for failing to vote. Critics claim this is hardly the mandate required to establish Mr Sis's credibility as a national leader tasked with the job of bringing stability and unity to the country. Nevertheless, as soon as the official results were declared on 3 June 2014, Saudi King Abdullah bin Abdulaziz hailed Sis's historic win, vowing continued support and calling upon countries to attend a donors' conference to help Egypt to overcome its economic difficulties. The Saudi establishment knows all too well that if Mr Sisi is unable to provide security and economic growth, it will not take too long for the Egyptian people to take to the streets again.

During the transitional period following the removal of Mr Morsi's government a massive influx of Gulf aid was pumped into the faltering Egyptian economy. The democratic elections that brought the Muslim Brotherhood to power represent a threat to the reign of unelected Sunni despots in the region. Consequently, a reversion of power to the military obviously plays into their hands. We are likely to see further restrictions on civil liberties as the former general tightens his grip on power. Supporters of the Muslim Brotherhood will predictably be subject to increasing repression, as will any form of dissent.

The crisis in Syria is frustratingly becoming a tough nut to crack. Misgivings by Russia and China in the United Nations Security Council over the motives of the United States, Britain, France and their NATO allies has allowed the Syrian regime to continue the mass killing of Syrian citizens with impunity. For some global players, saving human lives should not entail regime change with a military option. Despite UN monitors being on the ground to oversee the fragile ceasefire that purportedly took effect on 12 April 2012, the killings continued on both sides. The massacre that took place in the Syrian town of Houla, near Homs, in May 2012 and Syria's second city of Aleppo in July

2012, where the majority of casualties were innocent women and children, was a shameful tragedy for the international community, including the United Nations, for their ineptitude in failing to bring the warring parties to the negotiating table. It is no secret that both the Syrian Government and the opposition are being financially funded and militarily equipped by foreign powers, all with a vested interest in who controls Syria. It comes as no surprise therefore that the Syrian Foreign Minister, Walid al Muallem, while on a visit to Iran in July 2012, was reported by different media streams to have blamed Turkey, Qatar and Saudi Arabia ('Sunni Axis') for fuelling the rebellion across Syria, resulting in the failure of UN envoy Kofi Annan's peace plan. The mandate for UN Monitors was withdrawn at the end of August 2012. The Sunni Axis on the one side, and Iran and the Hezbollah in Lebanon on the other, appear to be jostling for influence in Syria, with analysts suggesting that the war within Syria is turning out to be a proxy war based on Shi'ite-Sunni sectarian differences exploited by Western powers. What is deeply disturbing with the Syrian Conflict is the large number of civilian casualties (around 100,000 according to UN estimates in July 2013) and the systematic destruction of Syria's infrastructure, not forgetting the 1.5 million refugees who have fled Syria to neighbouring countries, including Jordan and Lebanon, in addition to the many millions displaced internally in Syria. The country is imploding upon itself, as did Libya in 2011.

Strategically, a pro-Western Syrian government is indispensable for any future military strike against Iran, either by Israel or the West. Regrettably, stakes were raised in Syria's 18-month civil war when Turkey responded to shelling by Syrian forces in early October 2012 that killed five civilians in the Turkish border town of Akcakale. Though Turkey passed legislation authorizing its armed forces to carry out cross-border attacks against Syria, it did so without authorizing the involvement of Turkey's Western allies. It remains to be seen how far this proviso lasts. However, should Turkey, backed by NATO, go to war with Syria, the consequences will be catastrophic to Syria in terms of damage to its infrastructure, not to mention the substantial numbers of civilian deaths likely to result from such overwhelming military action. The car bomb blast in Lebanon's capital of Beirut on 19 October 2012 which resulted in several deaths, including that of Lebanese top intelligence official Wissam al-Hassan, gave cause for further concern, as the immediate public reaction was to blame the Syrian Government for carrying out the attack. In the meantime, following the collapse of Kofi Annan's peace initiative, international peace envoy Lakhdar Brahimi continued to tour the region, seeking to end the bloodshed in Syria. More often than not it is the situation on the ground that will dictate the chances of any peace initiative being successful.

It was anticipated in diplomatic circles that the stalemate would more than likely take a dangerous turn, resulting in direct military intervention by NATO if the Syrian regime used its alleged chemical weapons stockpiles to suppress its opponents. It was understood in the West that the Syrian government would be extremely reckless should it choose to do so and therefore, unlikely to rely on the support of Russia and China to veto a UN Resolution calling for armed intervention to unseat the Assad regime. However, despite reports in April 2013 that the nerve agent sarin was used (albeit on a small scale), the West, in particular the US and the United Kingdom, was cautious not to intervene directly militarily but rather subsequently made it public that they would be arming the Syrian opposition. At the

G8 Meeting held in Northern Ireland in June 2013, the Russian President reiterated that Moscow would not be breaching any law if it decided to arm the Syrian government. Russia had stated that it would be providing the Assad regime with advanced anti-aircraft missiles that would seriously undermine efforts to set up a no-fly zone. When, however, in August 2013 a deadly chemical attack was carried out on the outskirts of the capital Damascus in a civilian populated area, it caused an international outcry, with Britain and France calling for immediate military strikes against Assad's regime and blaming it for carrying out the attack. However, with MPs in the House of Commons voting against Britain being involved in military action against Syria, the US and France stepped up the pressure on Mr Assad by drumming up rhetoric in support of limited air strikes against military targets inside Syria. However, Russia, a strategic ally of the Syrian regime, opposed any such military strikes and brokered a solution to the impending crisis, persuading the Assad regime to commit itself to destroying its stockpile of chemical weapons. This is being carried out under the supervision of the Organisation for the Prohibition of Chemical Weapons (OPCW) as per UN Security Council Resolution 2118.

There is always the fear that should opposition forces get their hands on the government stockpiles of chemical and biological agents, this could prove extremely dangerous, given that reportedly certain 'extremist' elements have infiltrated the opposition forces on the ground.

Following on from the 'Geneva Communiqué' issued in June 2012, an international conference to find a political solution to the conflict in Syria began in Switzerland in January 2014, known as 'Geneva II'. Negotiations are decided not at the table but by the fortunes won in battle. The Assad regime will therefore press on with its fighting despite the talks and so will the rebel fighters. Difficult as it may sound, if a deal is to be reached that does not encompass Mr Assad, then he and his family must be given an exit plan while guaranteeing the Alawite community security in a post-Assad Syria. If not, should Assad step down, revenge attacks and summary executions against Mr Assad's family and the Alawite community will become widespread, resulting in nothing short of a massacre. The re-election of Mr Assad in June 2014 for another 7 years as President, however, is his way of sending a clear message to Western governments that any political settlement must encompass him in it.

Another serious cause of resentment lies in the allegation that occupation forces in Afghanistan and previously in Iraq, as well as the Israeli army operating in occupied territories in their quest for terrorists, have defiled the sanctity of Muslim homes. They are accused of smashing open the front doors of homes in the dead of night and dragging sleeping inmates, including women and children, out of their beds, rounding them up and terrorizing them with deafening shouts and pointing firearms at them close up. Children are traumatized, not knowing why these armed men have manhandled their frantic sisters and mothers and taken their brothers and fathers away from them, often for days and weeks, if not months. This raises the question of the number of instances when armed terrorists have actually been apprehended through these raids, while all the time radicalizing opinion against occupying forces.

The harrowing reports of abuse perpetrated on inmates at the Abu Ghraib prison in Baghdad by US servicemen and women caused hurt and anguish not only in Iraq but across the

Muslim world. Pictures of abuse released previously in 2004 showed a US private dragging a cowering Iraqi prisoner along the floor with a dog lead. Another showed her smoking a cigarette and pointing a mock gun at a naked prisoner's genitals. Other pictures released in 2004 included naked prisoners being subjected to terrifying taunts by dogs. So horrendous was the abuse that back in 2009, US President Barack Obama undertook to block publication of some graphic images allegedly involving US soldiers 'torturing Iraqi prisoners', fearing that they could provoke a serious backlash against American troops serving in Iraq and Afghanistan. Some of these pictures are reported to depict detainee nudity and images of detainees shackled, as well as pictures of weapons drawn and being pointed at detainees. Until full publication of such pictures is made we will not know their full nature.

In January 2014 a formal complaint was lodged with the International Criminal Court (ICC) in The Hague by Public Interest Lawyers (PIL) and the European Centre for Constitutional and Human Rights (ECCHR) calling for an investigation under Article 15 of the Rome Statute of the International Criminal Court into alleged war crimes involving systematic detainee abuse carried out by British troops serving in Iraq. The damning dossier draws on cases of more than 400 Iraqis, representing thousands of allegations of torture, cruel, inhuman and degrading treatment between 2003 and 2008. They range from 'hooding' prisoners to burning, electric shocks, sleep deprivation, noise bombardment, deprivation of food and water and cultural and religious humiliation. Other forms of alleged abuse include mock executions, sexual assault and threats of rape, death and torture.

The British MoD naturally denied that its troops

'systematically tortured' detainees, while the British Foreign Secretary, William Hague, exclaimed that there was no need for the ICC to investigate these allegations as many of them were either under investigation or had already been dealt with through public inquiries and the UK courts. In May 2014 the ICC nevertheless took the decision to conduct an initial investigation into such allegations of mistreatment. While some may argue that in the theatre of war it will be extremely naive to think that invading and occupying armies will not perpetrate excesses, this misses the point entirely. In this case, UK troops are required to operate within the parameters of international law in conflict situations with respect to detainees. This last point was reiterated by the British Attorney General, Dominic Grieve, who when completely rejecting the allegation of systematic abuse carried out by British armed forces in Iraq remarked that British troops operate to the highest standards in line with both domestic and international law, with the vast majority of the troops meeting that expectation while allegations of abuse were being comprehensively investigated. It will be interesting to observe how events unfold, particularly where Article 17 of the Rome Statute of the International Criminal Court provides that the ICC may only intervene where no effective investigation is being carried out by the national authorities.

Looking at Afghanistan, the year 2012 saw mass public uproar over photos and video depicting US Marines urinating on the corpses of 'insurgents', reports of the burning of the Holy Qur'an by US Forces at a US military base and the massacre of 16 unarmed civilians by Staff Sergeant Robert Bales and his immediate removal from the country, denying Afghan authorities any role in investigating the crime. These events have created a deep sense of hurt and contempt against occupation forces. Surely bridges need to be rebuilt to salvage the trust of the Afghan people, otherwise, the whole war effort will be lost.

An interesting but alarming twist on the situation in Afghanistan is the fact that in 2012 an increasing number of NATO troops have been killed by Afghan security forces in what has come to be known as 'green on blue', accounting for 15% of coalition deaths during that year.

The new front in 2013 was the military intervention in Mali by French troops to assist the Malian government to combat 'Islamist extremists' after rebel forces lost control of most of Mali's northern cities to Islamist forces. As the former colonial power it felt obliged to put boots on the ground when requested by the government to prevent Islamists from taking over the capital, Bamako. The attack on the Amenas gas field in Algeria focused world attention this time on the potential for North Africa becoming the next springboard for so called Islamist terrorists to attack Europe. With the UN Security Council backing the French intervention, it will be interesting to see how things develop. Without first crushing Islamist groups such as the Ansar Dine and the Movement for Oneness and Jihad in West Africa, we are unlikely to see a partition of Mali like Sudan.

The Norwegian Massacre of 22 July 2011 exposed a (pan European) neo-Nazi, ultra far right agenda based upon an irrational fear that lacks any real sustainable credibility. This extremist ideology threatens to undermine the democratic values and institutions upon which the European Union is based. If left unchecked, European Muslims will find themselves victims of their own Exodus in the future. It is not simply making a political issue of multiculturalism in an attempt to woo voters. It goes beyond that. Giving far-right propaganda a democratic platform will inevitably result in racial tensions.

There is no credible evidence to suggest that the vast majority of European Muslims are hell bent on establishing an Islamic caliphate in Europe. Far from it, the advocates of an Islamic caliphate would prefer the re-establishment of the caliphate in the Muslim Ummah. However, the insurmountable challenges in the way of re-establishing an Islamic caliphate in the Muslim Ummah based on democratic ideals make it clear that its realisation will not be without overcoming hurdles; though its establishment will no doubt act as a catalyst to achieving global peace as well as facilitating global commerce, acting as an effective counterweight to the global economic domination of China and India predicted by many economists by around 2035.

Post Cold War, ordinary Muslims are increasingly finding themselves being persecuted, whether in the form of ethnic cleansing, as in Bosnia, or foreign intervention to force regime change in order to secure energy supplies such as in Iraq, or lethal force being unleashed by tyrants in order to hang on to their reign on power, as evidenced by the Arab Spring.

When Muslims have suffered so much and endured such torment for so long it is ironic that they are losing the moral high ground. With Islam being demonized more often than not by Western media propaganda in the name of freedom of expression, Islam is perceived by the general population in the West as being synonymous with terrorism. This is giving rise to an undercurrent of tension within many national communities, threatening social cohesion. Party political rhetoric that multiculturalism is dead does not help! God forbid there should be another substantial terrorist attack in the West carried out by Al-Qaeda or its affiliates, for the backlash both by governments and non-Muslims against the general Muslim population there will be catastrophic. For instance, when on 22 July 2011 a fertilizer bomb went off in the Norwegian capital of Oslo in the vicinity of government buildings, followed by the massacre on Utoya Island that resulted in the death of 77 civilians, suspicion quickly fell upon so-called Muslim extremists, and there was an immediate initial backlash against Muslims living in Norway. It was only when it came to light that this was a terrorist act perpetrated by a non-Muslim, in fact by an ultra far right wing Norwegian extremist, namely Anders Behring Breivik, that the backlash died down. On 24 August 2012 Breivik was sentenced to 21 years' imprisonment' having been found sane and criminally responsible for his actions.

Global Muslims look to the political power structures in Saudi Arabia and the Middle East to embrace democratic norms and values respecting and enforcing individual civil rights and liberties. Despotic regimes in the Middle East, including Saudi Arabia, must give way to political pluralism in the interests of promoting democratic accountability and providing leadership to the Islamic World and placing it in an opportune position to face the global economic and political challenges that lie ahead. Saudi Arabia will always prove contentious for global Muslims as Islam's two holiest sites are situated on its western frontier.

Recent instances of 'terrorist attacks' against Western interests and its citizens since the tragic events of 9/11 include the Bali nightclub bombings on 12 October 2002, which killed 202 people, mostly foreigners, reportedly carried out by al-Qaeda-linked Jemaah Islamiyah. This was followed by the Madrid commuter train bombings on 11 March 2004 which killed 191 people just three days prior to the Spanish General Elections and was carried out by an al-Qaeda-inspired terrorist cell. On 07 July 2005 another alleged Al-Qaeda-inspired cell carried out a series of coordinated suicide attacks in London, targeting the public transport system during the morning rush hour and claiming the lives of 52 people.

We then have the coordinated shooting and bombing attacks reportedly carried out by Al-Qaeda linked Lashkar-e-Taiba (a Pakistani-based militant organization) across India's commercial capital, Mumbai, killing 164 people between 26 and 29 November 2008. The targets included the five-star hotels Oberoi Trident and the Taj Mahal Palace and Tower, which were frequented by Western tourists, as well as Nariman House, which is a Jewish centre. On 2 September 2013, alleged members of the Al-Qaeda linked al-Shabab attacked the opulent Westgate Shopping Mall in Kenya's capital city, Nairobi, also frequented by westerners, killing at least 62 people.

In addition to these, there have been a large number of thwarted 'terrorist attacks' against European and US targets since 9/11, the most prominent reportedly being the discovery of a plot in August 2006 to blow up several transatlantic flights. While Western leaders have insisted that there is no correlation between these acts of terror and events happening on the ground in Afghanistan, Israel and previously in Iraq, in reality however, global Muslims do not share the same view. As mentioned in the introduction, Muslims across the globe share a common psyche, though this manifests itself in different ways. The vast majority of the world's Muslims, it must be emphasized, condemn such criminal acts as nothing short of atrocities, distancing themselves from such a radical interpretation of Islam. In the meantime, Western media coverage has regrettably always branded these atrocities as 'Islamist'. Such sensationalist headlines give rise to suspicion and mistrust, threatening social cohesion within national communities in the West, while the vast majority of Muslims find such stereotyping offensive.

It would be inappropriate to leave this chapter without

taking a look at Osama bin Mohammed bin Awad bin Laden (commonly referred to as Osama bin Laden). He was born in Riyadh, Saudi Arabia on 10 March 1957, and his father, Mohammed bin Awad bin Laden, was the head of an extensive construction empire with close links to the Saudi royal family. Educated in Jeddah, in Saudi Arabia, Osama was inspired by the writings of Egyptian political activist Sayyid Qutub, who is widely credited as the father of so-called radical Islam. Upon the sudden death of his father in a plane crash, Osama bin Laden came into a substantial inheritance. Out of university he initially began working for the family company, but was incensed by the 1979 invasion of Afghanistan by the USSR. During the struggle to drive the Soviets out of Afghanistan, bin Laden, along with his Mujahideen allies, were more often than not branded by the Western powers as freedom fighters waging war against communist repression.

What turned the tide against Osama bin Laden was his violent reaction to the presence of the 800,000-strong American-led troops in Saudi Arabia at the invitation of the Saudi King following the invasion of Kuwait by Iraqi dictator Saddam Hussain's military machine in August 1990. The invasion prompted the Al-Sauds to fear for their very existence. If the Iraqi military machine could invade and occupy Kuwait there was nothing to stop them from invading Saudi Arabia. The Western powers feared this too. For them Saddam Hussain was unpredictable, and any invasion of Saudi Arabia would cause havoc to oil prices on the international market.

Osama bin Laden however, perceived the presence of foreign troops in Arabia as a violation of Islam's birthplace and its holy sites in Mecca and Medina, with the complicity of the Al-Saud ruling dynasty. For bin Laden there was no way to remove this foreign occupation other than through 'Jihad' against the US and its allies in the region. This anguish manifested itself as a long-term systematic campaign of bomb attacks on US targets, including the killing of 19 US soldiers in Dhahran, Saudi Arabia in 1996 and the simultaneous bombings of US Embassies in Nairobi in Kenya and Dar-es-Salaam in Tanzania in August 1998, killing more than 250 people and injuring more than 5000, as well as the suicide bomb attack in October 2000 on the US Navy destroyer USS *Cole* in Aden, killing 17 US servicemen.

It is reported that Al-Qaeda training camps were responsible for training the so-called insurgents/extremists who were active in fighting the Algerian military in the course of the civil war that erupted in Algeria in 1992 after the Islamic Salvation Front was denied electoral victory in the first round of general elections. It is also reported that Al-Qaeda operatives operated in Bosnia, Chechnya, Kashmir, as well as in the Philippines.

Osama bin Laden will forever be remembered in the West with contempt for allegedly orchestrating Al-Qaeda's most audacious attack on the West, which culminated in the tragic events of 9/11. Close to 3000 people died as a result of the attacks on the Twin Towers in New York and the Pentagon in Washington DC as well as the deaths of everyone on board the four airliners that were hijacked. A month after 9/11, when the Taliban government refused to hand over Osama bin Laden, the US and its allies, on 7 October 2001, launched an invasion of Afghanistan with the objectives of capturing Osama bin Laden dead or alive, destroying Al-Qaeda and removing the Taliban regime that was providing him sanctuary. Thirteen years on, US troops are still engaged in armed combat missions in Afghanistan against a Taliban-led insurgency. The US and the British have paid dearly in terms of troops who have lost their lives serving in Afghanistan. Sadly, the cost in terms of civilian loss of life has also been tragic. It was reported by Reuters (in an article by Daniel Trotta on 29 June 2011 with reference to a study conducted by the Brown University's Watson Institute for International Studies) that the number of civilian casualties as a direct consequence of the war in Afghanistan is well above 100,000. As to the financial cost to the US Treasury, it has been nothing less than substantial.

It was reported by Reuters in the same article that in the 10 years since US troops went into Afghanistan to effectively destroy Al-Qaeda following the 9/11 attacks, spending on the conflict had totalled between 2.3 trillion and 2.7 trillion dollars. As reported in *The Telegraph* (in an article by Thomas Harding on 28 July 2011 with reference to Ministry of Defence figures published in a Commons defence committee report), Britain had spent £18 billion in Afghanistan. While US President Barack Obama has committed to an end to US combat missions in 2014, there is no guarantee that the Taliban will be routed out of Afghanistan or subdued indefinitely.

In any event, on 1 May 2011, in a late-night appearance, President Obama announced to the World from the White House that US Navy SEALs had killed Osama bin Laden in his compound in Abbotabad in Pakistan. Violence begets violence! In hindsight, many in the Muslim world blame bin Laden for unwittingly giving Western Powers the leverage to introduce a new wave of imperialism in Muslim lands in the guise of 'War on Terror'. They allege that this has provided ideological cover for Western imperial policy to be projected militarily upon Muslim countries. The horrific 9/11 attacks were by extension the platform for the invasion and subsequent occupation of Iraq in 2003 and the continued occupation of Afghanistan. It provides the template behind the rationale for Western imperialistic policy: ie perpetual strife in the Middle East, the control of strategic oil supplies and the fragmentation of nations into their ethnic and religious fractions, such as the Shi'ite-Sunni tensions, not only in Iraq but much of that region also. They allege bin Laden was a 'godsend' for hawkish elements within the US Military establishment.

With the end of the Cold War and the disintegration of the USSR, strategic military policy has changed for Western powers. The threat to Western liberal democracy and capitalism is no longer communism but 'radical' Islam. Painfully though, the pro-liberal Muslim world, which has nothing to do with violent, radical Islam, is facing the brunt of Western imperial policy.

With the re-election of Barack Obama as President of the United States in November 2012 it was interesting to observe US foreign policy being somewhat reinvigorated, apparently taking on a more robust initiative in making some meaningful headway in bringing Israel and the Palestinians to the negotiating table, as well as the US relationship with the Muslim Ummah in light of the Arab Spring as it continues to unfold. On the Palestine issue, in its latest initiative, in July-August 2013, the US, under the stewardship of Secretary of State John Kerry, brought Palestinian and Israeli negotiators together to negotiate a 'final status' to the Palestinian-Israeli conflict. It was hoped that a solution would be reached within nine months. However, thorny issues such as Israeli settlement building in occupied territories, the 1967 borders, the status of East Jerusalem and the right of return of Palestinian refugees and their descendants dating back from Israel's 1948 war of independence, continue to undermine such a peace initiative. In fact six months on, each side was pointing the finger at the other for attempting to sabotage the talks.

In reality, it seemed that both Israeli and Palestinian leaders lacked the strong leadership and firm conviction to bring about such a peace. With so many stakeholders involved it is difficult for either of them to take decisive decisions. Consequently, the ultimatums for peace must be rooted not in US foreign policy but in the hopes and aspirations of the peoples of both Israel and Palestine. The political leadership requires a firm mandate from its peoples to negotiate an effective peace deal. However, the findings of the Zogby Research Services Poll that was carried out in the Middle East in August 2013 showed how very little confidence both Palestinians and Israeli citizens have in the new peace initiative.

The cycle of mistrust and violence between the two sides is sure to escalate with the failure of the US brokered peace initiative. Reportedly, Palestine is likely to seek full membership of the United Nations, as well as instituting proceedings under the Fourth Geneva Convention with the International Criminal Court over Israel's illegal settlement building. John Kerry had warned that if talks fail this may give rise to a third Palestinian uprising (Intifada) similar to the second uprising that broke out within a few months of the breakdown of the previous US-brokered peace talks back in July 2000. That lasted more than four years and resulted in the deaths of 4000 Palestinians. In the interests of state security Israel will naturally deploy its armed forces to quell any third Intifada.

How much more can Barack Obama achieve during the last years of his final term in office as US President against a staunchly pro-Israeli Congress remains to be seen. What is alarming for global Muslims and potentially damaging for renewed peace prospects is the move by Israeli right-wing politicians in February 2014 forcing a debate in the Israeli Knesset (Parliament) to enforce sovereignty over the Al-Aqsa mosque compound, which is currently being managed by an Islamic trust and administered by Jordan by virtue of the Jordan-Israeli peace treaty of 1994. Furthermore, eager to find evidence of what Israeli authorities believe to be ancient Jewish temples, excavation works are being carried out beneath the Old City of Jerusalem and the Al Aqsa mosque compound, posing a threat to the structural integrity of the sacred mosque. All the while elements within the Israeli political establishment wish to fulfil the 'Jewish prophecy' of building the Third Temple at the Al Aqsa mosque compound.

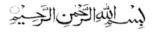

CHAPTER SEVEN

One Ummah: Revival of the Islamic Caliphate

In the context of re-establishing an Islamic Caliphate there is much debate about Islam and its compatibility with democracy. Importantly, it is imperative to determine what form of democracy should be adopted or exercised in a revived Caliphate. If we look at Western democracy we will observe that it comes in different shades of black and white. In the West, democracy is essentially a vehicle of government which represents a political superstructure requiring support from an economic substructure, namely free market economics and free enterprise. At the heart of this financial machine are predominantly the banks. Consequently when the banks began to collapse both in the United States and Europe in 2008, Western democracy was under threat. In an attempt to retain confidence in the markets and prevent civil unrest, governments desperately pumped billions in to bail out the banks. As a result increasing austerity measures were introduced by governments across Europe to overcome their respective deficits. Thanks to fragile currency markets and slow economic growth, the US and Europe are far from having overcome this financial crisis. Though Europe appears to have avoided for now a triple-dip recession, with the likelihood of increased job cuts in the public sector, a slow growth in the private sector, increased food and energy costs, repossessions of property and above pay-index inflation there is no place for complacency. Unless the vast majority of working class people feel the benefit of any economic recovery there will be a natural inclination to pin the blame for their economic woes on scapegoats.

All this is a recipe for increased social tensions. The successes of some far-right and anti-establishment political parties across the EU in the May 2014 European Parliamentary Elections, for example, illustrates an undercurrent of tension on immigration and the political union of Europe as a whole.

The protests that took place against government austerity measures in many European cities following the 2008 financial crisis, including those in Greece, Spain and the United Kingdom, were examples of frustration and disillusionment in attitudes towards governments. Though this was often denied and played down by respective governments, it is important to realise that when a government deploys state security forces to suppress widely participated legitimate protest with heavy-handed tactics the democratic legitimacy of that government is severely called into question. This can only undermine democratic values.

Robert Dahl in his work *A Preface to Economic Democracy* had argued that the unequal ownership of economic resources tends to concentrate political power in the hands of a few, which runs parallel to the Marxist critique of pluralist democracy. It raises the question whether in the 21st century we should contemplate political equality in the absence of economic equality.

Central to the concept of liberal democracy, which is often used interchangeably with pluralist democracy, is the principle that governments are elected on the basis of competition between political parties, a tolerance of wide-ranging political beliefs and electoral choice. A key feature of liberal democracy is the absence of a concentration of power. Instead there is a wide dispersal of political power among competing interests (including pressure groups), with a number of access points available to them. This ability for interest or pressure groups to press their demands and lobby government to influence policy establishes a channel of communication between them, creating a reliable link between the government and the governed. However, with austerity measures being rolled out by governments across Europe, trade unions as pressure groups are being prevented from carrying out their role effectively under a liberal democracy. In the United Kingdom for example, major Trade Unions, including the Public Commercial Services Union (PCS), are increasingly finding it difficult to defend working conditions, pay and pension rights for their members and prevent job losses despite resorting to lobbying members of parliament, organising substantial marches in London and holding lawful strikes after successfully balloting their members for industrial action.

The basis of representative democracy is holding regular, free and fair elections which are not only transparent but provide a level playing field for prospective candidates. The notion of 'one person one vote' gives the electorate a sense of purpose and belonging in determining the shape and direction of their future government. In real terms, however, the electorate only ever get to effectively exercise their democratic credentials by voting on Election Day every few years. In a parliamentary democracy when the party in power has a comfortable majority in the legislature, it becomes next to impossible to reverse subsequent policy if the government is determined to implement it no matter how unpopular it may prove to be. This ties in with the concept of 'strong and effective government' and the 'tyranny of the majority'. With respect to the United Kingdom, Lord Hailsham termed it an 'elective dictatorship'. Recent examples include Tony Blair's decision to take the United Kingdom to war over Iraq in 2003, which was widely opposed, with more than a million people marching in major cities across Britain, particularly London, on 15 February 2003. For Blair, his spin-doctors, much of his government and some media streams the decision to go to war amounted to the 'price of leadership and the cost of conviction'.

In terms of how representative governments are of the electorate, let us translate the percentages in the context of the United Kingdom. In the 2005 General Elections, for instance, Tony Blair's Government secured 35.2% share of the votes but 55% of the seats in the House of Commons, while the Conservative party secured 32.4% share of the vote but only 30% of the seats in the House of Commons. Again in 2010, the coalition government secured 59.1% share of the votes but secured 56% of the seats in the House of Commons. Much of this discrepancy comes down to the 'first past the post' electoral system employed at General Elections. Nevertheless, this must be examined against the backdrop that only 61.4% and 65.1% of the electorate turned out to vote in the 2005 and 2010 General Elections respectively. What that means is that in 2005 the Labour Government came to power with a mandate of

21.5% of the total electorate, while in 2010 the coalition Government came to power with a mandate of 38.5% of the total electorate. The extremely low turnout in the by-elections held in November 2012 for Manchester Central and Cardiff South and Penarth is of serious concern. It shows that the mainstream political parties failed to engage with the electorate so much so that only 18.5% of the electorate turned out to vote in Manchester Central (the lowest in peacetime Britain since the end of World War II). The general disillusionment with the mainstream parties has consequently manifested on a national level with UKIP securing a decisive win at the European Parliamentary Elections in May 2014 with 27.49% of the vote. UK voter apathy in the EU political system was represented by a disappointing turnout of 34.19%.

Electoral success in the United States has as much to do with campaign funding as it has to do with party policies. In the run-up to the 2012 US Presidential Elections, Republican candidate Mitt Romney and incumbent President Barack Obama received billions of dollars in campaign funding, much of it from corporate entities. Speaking at the Carter Center prior to the 2012 Election, former US President Jimmy Carter criticised the US electoral process, describing it as riddled with 'financial corruption' which dramatically favoured the elite. In contrast to a wide and democratic dispersal of power required by a liberal democracy, C. Wright Mills, in his illuminating account of power structures in the US, *The Power Elite*, claimed that political power is concentrated in the hands of a nexus of powerful groups including big corporate businesses, the US military and political stakeholders surrounding the Presidency. Consequently, this consortium of power elites shapes key policy decisions, including strategic economic, defence and foreign policy. Unions, small businesses and consumer lobbyists, on the other hand, are only ever able to exert any sort of real influence from the fringes of the policy process. He goes on to say that liberal democracy in the US is a sham.

In his critique of liberal democracy, Gaetano Mosca in his work *The Ruling Class* claims that with liberal democracies the resources or attributes that are necessary for political rule are always unequally distributed, and that a cohesive minority will always be in control of the levers of power, manipulating and controlling the masses, even in a parliamentary democracy. As Robert Michels puts it, this 'Iron Law of Oligarchy' permeates all democratic systems across Western Europe and the US. In terms of manipulating public perception, it is particularly dangerous when the different media streams are controlled by vested interests. Then again, the Media's ability to manipulate a story is dependent upon the naivety and complacency of the readership. In real terms politicians use the media to sell strategic policy issues to the public. Yet the media is only as powerful as its circulation.

Given the negative connotations surrounding Islam and democracy in the West, let us be bold enough to explore the term 'Islamic democracy'. It essentially comes down to the degree to which Islamic laws and ethics are incorporated into the affairs of state and their compatibility with preconceived notions of Western democracy. The critical question is whether Shari'ah should be the bedrock of government policy or co-exist with non-Shari'ah compliant legislation. While Malaysia has adopted or retained Islam as its state religion, Islamic law is not the only source of law. In Shi'ite-dominated Iran, however, Shari'ah is substantially integrated into the affairs of state, including legislation.

Also linked with the term 'Islamic democracy' is the degree of democratic participation in the policy-making process in the form of elected representation. Most Islamic majority states in South and South-East Asia, including Bangladesh, Pakistan, Indonesia and Malaysia, have elected legislative chambers. As a consequence of the Arab Spring, many Muslim majority states in the Middle East and North Africa will also be opting for elected representation in the legislative process.

If we use the concept of 'Shura' in a contemporary political setting, it can be argued that it refers to democratic processes to include democratic institutions and elections. Consequently, arbitrary governments and repressive political processes are contrary to political Islam. There is little conflict between (liberal) political Islam and political pluralism in its broad sense.

Let us now turn our attention to Bangladesh, Pakistan and Indonesia. Not only do they together, in terms of population and manpower, today represent a third of the Muslim Ummah, any revival of the Islamic Caliphate will likely to be influenced by events (past, present and future) in these countries. Bangladesh is not only an emerging economic power in South Asia but happens to be the third largest Muslim majority state in the Muslim Ummah after Indonesia and Pakistan. After achieving independence from West Pakistan following a bloody nine-month civil war which culminated in the surrender of 93,000 Pakistani troops of the Pakistan Eastern Command to the Allied Forces of India and Bangladesh (Mitro Bahini) represented by Lieutenant General Jagjit Singh Aurora in Dacca on 16 December 1971, Bangladesh is continuing its trek down the road to a functional democracy.

Let us briefly examine the major turning points. With the 4th amendment to the Constitution being passed through the

National Assembly in January 1975, President Sheikh Mujibur Rahman (the father of the nation) in the backdrop of the Cold War effectively sought to make Bangladesh a one-party state in the form of BAKSAL. Though the BAKSAL system was officially due to come into force on 1 September 1975, it failed to materialise following the bloody massacre of the President and most of his family at their Dhanmondi residence in Dacca (later renamed Dhaka) on the fateful morning of 15 August 1975 by junior military officers who were disillusioned by the direction Bangladesh was heading towards.

Then, following a series of coups and counter-coups after President Sheikh Mujibur Rahman's assassination, Major General Ziaur Rahman took over the reins of power as Chief Martial Law Administrator following the Sepoy Mutiny of 7 November 1975. With President Abusadat Mohammed Sayem subsequently relinquishing power in favour of Ziaur Rahman, the latter became a military president. Following presidential elections in June 1978, Ziaur Rahman sought to give his presidency and political ambition democratic legitimacy. The National Assembly of the Republic was brought back to life following general elections in 1979. A heavy question mark hangs over the integrity of these elections. Subsequently, on the morning of 30 May 1981, President Ziaur Rahman was assassinated at the Circuit House in Chittagong in an abortive military coup.

Less than a year later, on 24 March 1982, Lieutenant General Hussain Muhammad Ershad took power in a bloodless coup from President Abdus Sattar (who was elected after Ziaur Rahman's assassination), suspending the constitution and imposing martial law. H.M. Ershad, like Ziaur Rahman, later became President of Bangladesh, forming his own political party, namely the Jatiya Party, as opposed to Ziaur Rahman's Bangladesh Nationalist Party (BNP). President Ershad, however, was forced to resign on 6 December 1990 following a mass upsurge protesting against farce elections, widespread corruption and years of misrule. Since then Bangladesh has had both Sheikh Mujib's Awami League and Ziaur Rahman's BNP securing power through elections conducted under caretaker governments, the former led by Sheikh Hasina Wajed, daughter of Sheikh Mujibur Rahman and the later by Begum Khaleda Zia, widow of Ziaur Rahman. The acrimonious relationship between the two political rivals has done little to consolidate democratic tolerance. Such democratic credence has been called into question with the tenth Parliamentary elections being held on 5 January 2014 under a cabinet led by Sheikh Hasina supervised by the Election Commission.

The Awami League and the BNP both accuse each other of tainting the judicial system by packing the courts with men of their own political persuasion. Regrettably, the Higher Courts have not escaped this controversy either. So much so that the Awami League refused to participate in parliamentary elections under a caretaker government coming at the end of the BNP-led Government's term in office in October 2006, accusing the then Chief Justice of being pro-BNP. As recently as December 2011, the Bangladesh Institute of Law and International Affairs (BILIA) reportedly claimed that the Awami League-led government appointed 52 judges to the Higher Courts in the three years since coming to power, while the previous BNP-led government appointed 45 judges to the Higher Judiciary. In the absence of due process of law in the selection process, keynote speakers expressed their concerns over the transparency and democratic accountability of higher judicial appointments.

Meanwhile, the military establishment has always kept a keen eye on political developments, again directly interfering in the country's political affairs between January 2007 and December 2008 following the widespread violence that gripped the country after the opposition alliance, led by the Awami League, refused to contest the January 2007 General Elections under the caretaker government of President Ijajuddin Ahmed. Sheikh Hasina was subsequently sworn in as Prime Minister in January 2009 following the Awami League's landslide victory in the December 2008 General Elections.

Freedom of the Press in Bangladesh is not without its dangers. Journalists have gone missing and have even been killed in broad daylight, not to mention manhandling by the police. Also of concern is the closing down of different media channels which are viewed as particularly hostile and party-politically motivated against the government. For example, the BNP-led government of Khaleda Zia went all guns blazing against Ekushey TV when it was elected to power in October 2001, dragging the TV channel through the courts. Again, after the Awami League-led government assumed power in January 2009 it is alleged to have forced the closure of the private television channels Channel-1, Diganta and Islam TV, as well as newspaper publications, such as Amar Desh, with its editor, Mahmadur Rahman being arrested and jailed as recently as April 2013 on charges of sedition and breach of the ICT Act 2006 as well as inciting violence and religious tension.

The relatively peaceful elections conducted by the Election Commission in the four city corporations in June 2013 had been argued by the ruling party as evidence that free and fair elections can be conducted under an Awami League-led government. However, the victory by pro-BNP candidates in all four city corporations had been highlighted by the BNP as a vote of no confidence in the current government and a declaration by the people of Bangladesh that they wanted the upcoming General Elections to be held under a neutral caretaker government. With both main political parties claiming the moral high ground, they appeared more and more entrenched, if not polarised in their outlook. Consequently, democracy in Bangladesh faced its biggest challenge at the end of 2013, when the Awami League led-government came to the end of its term in office. The main opposition party at the time, the BNP, had insisted that parliamentary elections be held under a neutral caretaker government. The ruling Awami League, however, had continually reiterated that the General Election would be held under the incumbent cabinet, albeit a smaller cabinet (through supervision of the Election Commission) and not under a caretaker government. Previously, in June 2011, the 15th amendment to the Constitution scrapped the provision for a neutral caretaker government to oversee General Elections.

Following weeks of violent strikes and demonstrations, the BNP boycotted the parliamentary elections, but the Awami League-led Government nevertheless went ahead with the General Election on 5 January 2014 without entering any sort of meaningful dialogue with the opposition, which tested the democratic will of the people to its core. Bangladesh experienced political fallout, with the Awami League-led Government being accused of orchestrating the suppression of opposition party political activity through, for example, the mass arrest of political activists, media censorship, alleged extra-judicial killings and abductions immediately prior to the elections. In this context, what Bangladesh needs is a widely perceived impartial and strong Election Commission with the necessary legal powers to conduct free, fair and transparent parliamentary elections. The main political parties in Bangladesh must develop a culture of political tolerance. If this cannot be expected from the current generation of leaders, then hopefully the next generation of political leaders will exhibit such democratic credentials.

The Awami League-led government has placed the trial of collaborators of the Pakistan Army during Bangladesh's war of independence from West Pakistan high on its political agenda. Mass demonstrations began in earnest in February 2013, at Shahbag, in the capital, Dhaka, and then spread to the rest of the country, participators demanding the death penalty for those convicted. This demand then went a step further, demanding the abolition from the political arena of the Jamaat-e-Islam, accusing them of being opposed to the Liberation War, as well as being violent religious fundamentalists. There were also calls to banish religious-based politics in Bangladesh altogether. It seemed that a deliberate ploy was being hatched to orchestrate a showdown between secularist and Islamist forces. As a consequence, the Capital and other cities witnessed strikes and violent clashes with the police.

The government and its spin-doctors blamed the violence on anti-liberation forces and violent religious extremists. The then main opposition party BNP however, insisted that the events in Shahbag were nothing but a political ploy by the government to divert public opinion from allegations of government corruption and misrule. The brutal crackdown by the security forces on supporters of 'Hefazote Islam' in the early hours of May 6, 2013 in the capital, Dhaka, that resulted in several deaths, raises grave concerns over lack of civil liberties and political tolerance. The crackdown was a hasty reaction by the authorities over concerns that the demonstrations that were attended by tens of thousands of Hefazote Islam supporters could turn into a formidable challenge to the government if BNP activists joined in. (Hefazote Islam's appearance on the political platform was a spin-off to the Shahbag Demonstrations.)

Many argue that given the notoriety associated with Jamaat-e-Islam in Bangladesh, restricting it would help a new generation of progressive Muslim leaders to enter the political spectrum, the only caveat being that this new wave of political leaders does not appear to be reactionary. If Jamaat-e-Islam is to endure then it needs to rebrand itself with a new charter which, among other things, explicitly denounces violence, respects and recognises the independence and sovereignty of Bangladesh in condemning the genocide of 1971 and works towards promoting interfaith dialogue, with its main focus on seeking political office by participating in the electoral process.

We can nevertheless draw inspiration from the demonstrations in Shahbag in the sense that a similar upsurge against the political 'old guard' will indeed provide the platform for much needed cross-party political reform. It will be interesting to see how things pan out, as it may very well provide a blueprint for what will happen in the rest of the Muslim Ummah as the new generation of middle class, particularly in the Arab World, wrestle with their religious roots in coming to terms with the 21st century.

Not only is Bangladesh my ancestral home, I have had the unique opportunity to observe first-hand her transition from a dictatorship to a fledgling democracy and its aftermath. The turbulent history of Bangladesh is reminiscent of many Muslim majority states which have been marred by corruption, farcical elections, misrule and an overbearing military. The Arab Spring that swept North Africa and parts of the Middle East was a reaction to similar circumstances.

Pakistan, the second largest Muslim majority state in the Muslim Ummah, has also had a chequered history of military intervention in state politics. Both General Zia-ul-Haq and General Parvez Musharraf seized political power from elected governments. In July 1977, General Zia-ul-Haq had Prime Minister Zulfikar Ali Bhutto arrested, dissolving the National Assembly together with all provincial assemblies and suspending the constitution. In October 1999, senior army officers loyal to General Parvez Musharaf arrested Prime Minister Nawaz Sharif in a coup d'état. Interestingly, both generals have proved useful to the West, in particular the United States. General Zia-ul-Haq proved instrumental in assisting the US-supported Mujahideen in its war with Soviet Forces in Afghanistan. Later General Parvez Musharraf proved to be a useful ally in the United States-led 'War on Terror', particularly against the Taliban in Afghanistan. Mr Asif Ali Zardari (widower of former Prime Minister Benazir Bhutto and son-in-law of former Prime Minister Zulfikar Ali Bhutto) was elected President of Pakistan in September 2008. It was widely reported in the Pakistan media that Mr Zardari was tainted by allegations of corruption. Following the 18th Amendment to the Constitution the office of President was stripped of key political powers previously invoked by former Presidents, including the power to dissolve Parliament and to dismiss the Prime Minister. While the 19th and 20th Amendments to the Constitution have strengthened the position of the office of the Prime Minister, nevertheless, in June 2012, Mr Yousuf Raza Gillani was ousted and disqualified retrospectively from the office of Prime Minister by the Supreme Court of Pakistan, which had found Mr Gillani guilty of contempt of court for failing to implement its earlier ruling directing the government to reopen the graft cases against President Zardari. Mr Gillani was succeeded by Mr Raja Parvez Ashraf. In January 2013 in what analysts suggest being a result of a power struggle between the judiciary and the PPP-led government, the Supreme Court ordered the arrest of Prime Minister Raja Parvez Ashraf over allegations of corruption while he was Minister for Water and Power in 2010. While this did not necessarily lead to his resignation, the timing was somewhat precarious as Pakistan was due for elections later on in the year.

Pakistan is a country blighted with sectarian violence between different Muslim sects, often with mosques being bombed. With the US drone strikes on the Pakistani-Afghan border, Pakistan is gradually descending into deeper political and financial crisis. With Nawaz Sharif again becoming the Prime Minister following General Elections held in May 2013, he will no doubt face testing times in tackling a potential Taliban resurgence following the expected withdrawal of US forces from Afghanistan in 2014. In this context, it is imperative that the US strike up some sort of meaningful and constructive dialogue with the Taliban. Such a move was initiated in June 2013 in what US officials called 'peace and reconciliation' talks. Meanwhile, Mr Sharif's tact in dealing with the Pakistan military establishment will be interesting to observe.

A former military general also ruled Indonesia, the largest Muslim majority state in the Muslim Ummah, for more than 30 years. Major General Suharto came to power in the aftermath of an abortive coup in 1965 accredited to communist elements. He became President in March 1967 and ruled with an iron hand until his resignation in May 1998. Under pressure from the United States and the International Monetary Fund (IMF) to introduce radical reforms following the economic collapse in 1997, coupled with defections of his Party faithful and mass student protests, President Suharto's fate was sealed. For the younger generation, alongside new-found political freedoms, economic emancipation is equally important. The same can be said for Bangladesh and Pakistan.

The above military dictators turned Presidents all believed that civilian rule was weak and that their countries were not ready for democratic rule. Regrettably, however, despite the fall of these despots, the average citizen is still yet to substantially benefit from these new fledgling democracies. These countries have a long trek and many hurdles to overcome before they can become mature democracies. Decades of corruption has embedded itself in all spheres of administration, making it endemic, while all three countries today are facing an increasing influence of radical Islam with the military in Bangladesh reportedly claiming that it foiled a coup planned by fanatical officers in January 2012. It will be interesting to observe what direction these titans of the Muslim Ummah take. Of the three, Indonesia is nevertheless, poised to be a 'top ten economy', while Bangladesh is making sound economic progress, driven particularly by private sector engagement with substantial exports of ready-made garments to European and American markets as well as the large foreign remittance it receives from its expats. Sandwiched between the emerging economic super-powers, India and China, in the not-too-distant future Bangladesh is conveniently placed to achieve considerable economic prosperity, provided the political leadership in Dhaka can set aside their acrimonious relationship and work together for the prosperity of the country.

Any notion to re-establish an Islamic caliphate based upon

the concept of a unitary state will more than likely prove self-defeating and only breed extremism. Today the Muslim Ummah is divided among 50 plus nation-states forged in large part as a struggle against colonial rule and exploitation. The advocates of an Islamic caliphate need to respond effectively to the contemporary global political situation. Core characteristics could include a common citizenship; a single currency; a Federal Reserve Bank but operating on the principles of Islamic Shari'ah; a single customs union; a representative central political authority respecting the national, political and in parts the legal sovereignty of individual member states much like the EU; an independent legal entity sitting as the highest appellate body on the interpretation of (Federal) legislation and a common foreign and defence policy similar to the US Federal system. The West and particularly Israel have nothing to lose from the establishment of an Islamic caliphate, and everything to gain from it in terms of regional security and economic cooperation. The bedrock upon which the caliphate should be re-established however, to give it any chance of success, can only be the practice of political pluralism among the Member States.

As a consequence of the military's involvement in state affairs both past and present, not only in South Asia but also in the Middle East and North Africa, it is imperative for the proponents of a revived Islamic caliphate to first assess and evaluate what role the armed forces should play. It would be a wasted effort for a revived Caliphate to be hijacked by the military 'Old Guard' sitting on the fringes of political power and shadowing elected governments. In the interests of securing a viable Islamic caliphate, the military's involvement in the democratic make-up of participating Member States must be evaluated. Again, much like the North Atlantic Treaty

Organisation (NATO), it would also be important to consider whether there should be a standing military force brought under a (democratic) central command structure to face external aggression and to keep the peace among participating states. More importantly, it is imperative to determine what form of democracy will be exercised in a revived Caliphate, given that democracy comes in different shades as highlighted above.

It goes without saying that a revived Islamic caliphate must operate under a binding legal framework. This could take the form of enabling Treaties similar to the E.U. model and/or a constitution based on the U.S. Federal system. The proponents of a revived Caliphate should have a realistic blueprint or roadmap against which to form strategic policy objectives otherwise all efforts will be self-defeating. We notice organisations working actively in many Muslim countries advocating the revival of an Islamic caliphate but often resorting to non-pragmatic and sometimes radical methods. This is both non-productive and unfortunate. At the very heart of a revived Caliphate is the mindset of global Muslims. They must believe in its implementation and appreciate its financial benefits in terms of economic empowerment and security. At the same time, policy-makers within Muslim states must aspire to such a revival. In this context, the Arab Spring that started in 2011 as a rebellion against despotic rule is a step in the right direction, providing of course the remnants of the old regimes fail to continue to pull the levers of power in the shadows of new elected governments. Furthermore, the new constitutions must reflect a desire to uphold the core values of a united caliphate. Then again, like the EEC, a revived Islamic caliphate can initially take the form of a forum-fostering economic cooperation between founding participating countries subsequently taking on a more political role accommodating Muslim countries wishing to join in.

While many regard the capitulation of the Ottoman Empire on 30 October 1918 as the demise of the Islamic Caliphate and seek a revival, it would be counterproductive if advocates in favour of a revived caliphate strive for a return to an Ottoman-style caliphate based on its last days.

Among other things, an Islamic caliphate should ensure that all citizens of the caliphate are equal under the law irrespective of their religious beliefs. They must be protected by their respective national constitutions supplementing a Charter of Civil Liberties adopted as Federal law with treaty articles enforceable in domestic courts with the final appeal to the highest appellate (Federal) court. A revived Islamic caliphate, in the interests of promoting economic stability in the Middle East and the wider Muslim world, should aggressively pursue a peace treaty with Israel by mutually-agreed land swaps, reaching a consensus on the right of return and the status of the holy city of Jerusalem among other things. With respect to Jerusalem, a possible way forward could be establishing a principality within Jerusalem encompassing Islam's holy sites as the capital of a viable independent state of Palestine. This goal to seek peace with Israel resulting in a viable two-state solution may form part of the preamble to a Federal constitution or enabling Treaty Articles if the Islamic Caliphate is based on the EU model. Like Europe and the US, Israel is facing economic hardship, with a relatively substantial percentage of its GDP going on defence spending. In early September 2011, after 50 days of protest, almost half a million Israelis marched across Israel demanding social justice, a lower cost of living and a clear government response to the concerns of an increasingly squeezed middle class. The biggest march was in Tel Aviv, where almost 300 thousand marched. In Jerusalem there was an unprecedented 50 thousand strong protest march. If we take this in context, Israel's population is only 7.7 million. The marches were well attended by students and young Israelis, which hopefully indicates that the next generation of Israelis will transform the landscape of Israeli politics and work to achieve the economic emancipation of all Israeli citizens by proactively pursuing peace and not war.

The recent discovery of major gas fields off its north Mediterranean coast is likely to reduce Israel's dependency on gas imports primarily from Egypt. It is reported that it may even turn Israel into a natural gas exporting country. This may increase its political leverage with neighbouring countries, hopefully enabling working partnerships for economic emancipation.

The nature of warfare is set to change in the foreseeable future. Conventional war, as we know it, is now being recognised by Western governments as no longer financially sustainable or logistically viable. Western governments are likely to rein in their conventional military expenditure because of what appears to be a long-term economic downturn. Unmanned warfare is likely to be the emphasis placed by Western military strategists, in the form of cyber warfare such as the Stuxnet virus attack on Iran's nuclear programme in 2010, as well as drone attacks as the ones currently being used on suspected Taliban targets on the Afghan-Pakistan border. The increased use of readily deployable armed strike forces similar to those involved in the assassination of Osama bin Laden appears to be a preferred tactical initiative.

Financial warfare in the form of crippling economic

sanctions is presumably set to stay high on the agenda. We can see this in the form of Western sanctions on Iran, which include the EU ban on all oil imports from Iran imposed in July 2012, coupled with US measures against Iran's Central Bank in response to Iran's alleged uranium enrichment programme. Another stark example is the increased Western sanctions imposed in 2012 on Syria in response to atrocities carried out by the Syrian regime against its citizens. The financing and arming of rebellions by Western powers against 'rogue governments', as we saw in Libya in 2011 and subsequently in Syria, evidently appears to be a new military strategy.

The nuclear option is always there as a last resort for the West, which is why it is so important for Western governments that developing countries, particularly Muslim countries, do not attain nuclear weapons. Pakistan is the only Muslim country to be internationally recognised as possessing a nuclear arsenal, predictably to be used in case of nuclear conflict with its age-old adversary, India. It is very unlikely Pakistan will ever have reason to deploy its nuclear arsenal against any other country. Conflict between the two neighbours is also likely to draw China into the fray. Consequently, any nuclear exchanges in South Asia will be catastrophic for the emerging economic superpowers. Whatever progress India and Pakistan have achieved since their independence from British colonial rule would be thrown away. China too will suffer catastrophically.

A revived Islamic caliphate should be in a position to effectively respond to this change in military stratagem by Western powers to defend itself against hawkish military interests and vested stakeholders.

Many governments in Muslim majority countries, including those in South Asia and the Middle East, are enacting and enforcing so-called anti-terror laws with the principal aim of silencing party political opposition, and in the process, as an added benefit to vested stakeholders, undermining the chances of any Islamic revival. The consequence of this is disillusionment among the young, who resort to lapses in moral judgement, fostering acts of criminality. Many of these countries are infested with rampant corruption in all spheres of socio-economic life and ruled by elected political dynasties or hereditary despots. Either way, they are backed by an opportunist class of elites and an over-zealous military.

It is the radical interpretation of Islam as a violent political response to perceived victimisation of the Muslim Ummah that is at odds with Western foreign policy. It can be argued that there is substance in such perceptions when, for instance, US President Barack Obama, in January 2013 at a joint White House press conference with Afghan President Hamid Karzai, made it abundantly clear that despite the US troops' withdrawal in 2014, it would nevertheless keep a military presence in Afghanistan, albeit under the terms of a bilateral security agreement. Following on from this, in May 2014 the US President announced plans that 9800 US troops would remain in Afghanistan at the end of 2014 to assist Afghan forces to fight remnants of Al Qaeda. With outgoing President Hamid Karzai refusing to sign a security deal with the US, the candidates standing for the upcoming presidential elections are reported to have indicated their willingness to sign such a deal. With the US continuing to retain a strong naval presence in Bahrain, some will therefore seek to argue that the Muslim Ummah is under siege from US imperial policy. Whether that be the case or not, surely the Muslim Ummah has been substantially weakened in terms of the political unrest in Iraq, the ongoing Taliban threat in Afghanistan, the apparent failure of the Arab

Spring as evidenced by the military coup in Egypt, the ongoing crises in Syria, the suppression of democratic protests in Bahrain and the continued reign of despots in the Middle East.

The current situation in Syria and Iraq is nothing short of breathtaking in terms of the potential threat to stability in the Middle East. What the insurgents in the shape of the Islamic State of Iraq and Syria (ISIS) have done in capturing major Iraqi cities, including the second largest city, Mosul, in June 2014 with terroritorial gains spreading from Syria into Iraq, is the real potential of setting up a political entity in the form of a transnational Islamic Caliphate. ISIS has indeed taken maximum adavantage of the civil war in Syria and the Sunni resentment in Iraq against the authoritarian rule of Shi'ite Prime Minister Nouri al-Maliki. It would not be out of place, therefore, to argue that ISIS represents a threat to Shi'ite influence in the region and consequently, is likely to be cautiously tolerated by Sunni Despots. Indeed, ISIS may very well prove to be a double-edged sword. Therefore, the longer the regional powers delay in taking action against the insurgency the more formidable an antagonist ISIS will present itself.

Should Baghdad fall to ISIS, the Assad Regime in Syria will find it extremely difficult to retain its grip on power, in which case the Syrian Regime will not be fighting an insurgency but a political entity in the form of a Caliphate. In the worst case scenario, Iraq and Syria will splinter and sectarian wars in the region will become more prevalent, leaving a deeply-divided Muslim Ummah in its wake.

It must be stressed that any attempt to re-establish an Islamic Caliphate through violence and destruction has the potential of having serious consequences in terms of its sustainability. This is particularly so if a narrow narrative of Shari'ah is enforced on the populace with an iron hand. The absence of democratic norms and practices will give rise to despotic leaders who are unaccountable to any legitimate democratic processes.

Despite its many shortcomings democracy should nevertheless be the preferred norm. It need not necessarily have to be based on the Western model and certainly not enforced upon Muslim countries by the Western military machine. Though the notion of living in a democracy gives the populace a sense of engagement in the political process, in reality, however, in states exhibiting democratic credentials supported by capitalist infrastructure, the establishment and ruling elite will always pull the levers of power. This is evidenced by the socio-economic make-up of those elected to their National legislatures, which is true of all democratic countries but more so in countries riddled with corruption. A revived caliphate must therefore be able to reconcile key democratic values with competing interests within the spirit of Islamic jurisprudence.

As a precursor to a revived Islamic caliphate it would be befitting to have a day of remembrance and prayer for Muslims killed since the end of the Second World War as a result of persecution, whether that be by their own tyrannical rulers as political dissidents, ethnic cleansing of Muslim minorities, such as the genocide committed against Muslim Bosniaks, or the countless external invasions and occupations that have resulted in the violent deaths of tens of thousands of non-combatants. A highlight of the day can be a two-minute silence observed by Muslims across the globe marked by a simple prayer for those who have lost their lives as a consequence of persecution. The day could aptly be called 'Martyrs' Day' and commemorated once a year, preferably on the 'Day of Ashura' whose significance in Islam can hardly be underestimated. This Remembrance Day will signify to the world that Muslims across the globe stand united as one Ummah in their remembrance of those Muslims who have died from persecution, as well as resisting their own transgressions.

CHAPTER EIGHT

The End of Time -
The Hour Glass Shatters

The knowledge of the Final Hour is with ALLAH alone. This is narrated in the following verses of the Holy Qur'an:

■ Chapter 7, Al-A'raf, Verse 187: *"They ask thee about the (final) Hour — when will be its appointed time? Say: "The knowledge thereof is with my Lord (alone): None but He can reveal as to when it will occur. Heavy were its burden through the Heavens and the Earth. Only, all of a sudden will it come to you." They ask thee as if thou wert eager in search thereof: Say: "The knowledge thereof is with ALLAH (alone), but most men know not."*

■ Chapter 31, Luqman, Verse 34: *"Verily the knowledge of the Hour is with ALLAH (alone). It is He who sends down rain, and He who knows what is in the wombs. Nor, does any one know what it is that he will earn tomorrow. Nor does any one know in what land he is to die. Verily with ALLAH is full knowledge and He is acquainted (with all things)."*

- Chapter 33, Al-Azhab, Verse 63: *"Men ask thee concerning the Hour: Say, "The knowledge thereof is with ALLAH (alone)":And what will make thee understand? It may be that the Hour is nigh!"*

- Chapter 41 Fussilat, Verse 47: *"Unto Him is referred (All) knowledge of the Hour. And no fruit burst out of its sheath, nor does a female conceive nor bring forth, but with His Knowledge. The Day that ALLAH will calleth unto them, "Where are the Partners (Ye attributed) to Me?" They will say, "We do assure Thee that not one of us is a witness for them."*

And the Final Hour is surely to happen, there is no doubt thereof as stated in the following verses of the Holy Qur'an.

- Chapter 20, TaHa, Verse 15: *"Lo! The Hour is surely coming. But I will keep it hidden, that every soul may be rewarded for that which it striveth (to achieve)."*

- Chapter 22, Al-Hajj, Verse 7: *"And verily the Hour will come: There can be no doubt about it, or about (the fact) that ALLAH will raise up all those who are in the graves."*

- Chapter 34, Sabah, Verse 3-4: *"Those who disbelieve say, "Never to us will come the Hour", say, "Nay! But most surely, by my Lord, it will come upon you; - by Him Who knows the unseen, - From Whom is not hidden an atoms weight in the Heavens or on earth: Nor is there anything less than that or greater, but it is in a clear Record: That he may reward those who believe and work deeds of righteousness: for them is forgiveness and a sustenance most gracious."*

- Chapter 40, Al-Ghafir, Verse 59: *"The Hour will certainly come: Therein there is no doubt: Yet most men believe not."*

While the exact timing of the Final Hour is not specifically mentioned in the Holy Qur'an, nevertheless there are signs mentioned in many Ahadith by which the devout may foresee the coming of the Hour. The Holy Qur'an does however, describe the Final Hour in apocalyptic terms in Chapter 81, At-Takwir, verses 1-14: *"When the sun (with its spacious light) is folded up; when the stars fall, losing their lustre; when the mountains vanish; when the she-camels, ten months with young are left unattended; when the wild beasts are herded together; when the oceans boil over with a swell; when the souls are sorted out (like with like); when the female (infant) that was buried alive is questioned – for what crime she was slain; when the Scrolls are laid open; when the sky is torn away; when the Blazing Fire (hell) is kindled to fierce heat; and when the Garden is brought nigh; (Then) every soul will know what it has put forward."*

It is narrated from Abu Huraira (Sahih Al-Bukhari, Volume 1, Book 2, Belief, Hadith Number 47) that one day while the Prophet Muhammad was sitting with a group of people, a Bedouin came to the Prophet and asked Him about Iman and Islam. Then he asked, "O Messenger of ALLAH, when will the Hour be established? The prophet replied, *"The answerer has no better knowledge than the questioner, but I will tell you about its portents. When a slave (lady) gives birth to her master; when the shepherds of black camels start (boasting and) competing with others in the construction of higher buildings. The Hour is one of the five things which no-one knows except ALLAH."* Then the prophet is reported to have recited Chapter 31, Luqman, Verse 34, mentioned above.

After the Bedouin took his departure from the Prophet, He said to those gathered around Him, "Call him back", but when the people went out to call him, the Bedouin was nowhere to be found. The Prophet then said, *"That was Jibrael (Gabriel), who came to teach the people their religion."*

Other Sahih Hadith pertaining to the Final Hour include the following:

It is reported from Anas (Sahih Al-Bukhari,Volume 1, Book 3, Knowledge, Hadith Number 81) that the Prophet said, *"Among the signs of the Hour are the following: (Religious) knowledge will decrease and ignorance will prevail; fornication (illegal sexual intercourse/having sex with someone not married to) will be prevalent; the number of women will increase, until one man will look after fifty women."* By knowledge, here we can assume the knowledge and wisdom in the Truth of Tauhid and all that it stands for.

Again, it is narrated by Abu Huraira in (Sahih Al-Bukhari, Volume 9, Book 88, Afflictions and the End of War, Hadith Number 237) that the Prophet said, *"The Hour will not be established till: (1) two big groups fight each other whereupon there will be a great number of casualties on both sides and they will be following one and the same religious doctrine, (2) about thirty Dajjals (liars) appear, and each one of them will claim that he is ALLAH's Messenger, (3) the religious knowledge is taken away (by the death of religious scholars), (4) earthquakes will increase in number (5) time will pass quickly, (6) trials and afflictions will appear, (7) Al-Harj (i.e. killing) will increase, (8) wealth will be in abundance ... so abundant that a wealthy person will worry lest nobody should accept his Sadaqa, and whenever he will present it to someone, that person (to whom it is offered) will say, 'I am not in need of it,' (9) the people compete with one another in constructing high buildings, (10) a man when passing by a grave of someone will say, 'Would that I were in his place,' (11) and till the sun rises and the people will see it (rising in the west) they will all believe (embrace Islam) but that will be the time when: (As ALLAH said), 'No good will it do to a person to believe then, if he (or she) believed not before, nor earned good (by performing deeds of righteousness) through his (or her) Faith.'*

And the Hour will be established while two men spreading a garment in front of them but they will not be able to sell it, nor fold it up; and the Hour will be established when a man has milked his she-camel and has taken away the milk but he will not be able to drink it; and the Hour will be established before a man repairing a tank (for his livestock) is able to water (his animals) in it; and the Hour will be established when a person has raised a morsel (of food) to his mouth but will not be able to eat it."

These portents of the Final Hour are often referred to as the lesser or early signs. It is not uncommon - in fact it is convenient - to adopt an escapist perspective on the Final Hour, denying any possibility of its relevance in our lifetime. However, even the Prophet Muhammad did not know of its exact timing. We are already witnessing many of the lesser signs of the Final Hour. Many have come to pass; some are ongoing, while others are yet to happen. Also among the lesser signs is the rejection of the moral values of the Holy Qur'an, where despite the fact that the Holy Qur'an is read, the knowledge and wisdom it contains will not be practiced; religion will be used as a means for profit and gain; worship performed for show; the mosques being full of people but they will be empty of righteous guidance; so-called Muslims (hypocrites) will be in the majority, while real scholars and sincere Muslims will be in the minority. Liars will be believed at the expense of truthful people. Gains will be shared out only among the rich, with no benefit for the poor. Furthermore, unrepresentative regimes will enforce tyrannical rule.

Among the major signs, they include the emergence of the Dajjal (the false Messiah), the appearance of the Mahdi, the rightly guided leader of the Muslim Ummah who will fight the tribulations of the Dajjal; the second coming of Isa (Jesus), son of Mary who will kill the Dajjal; the havoc created by the 'tribes' of Ya'jooj and Ma'jooj (Gog and Magog); the three Landslides, one in the east, one in the west and one in the Arabian Peninsula; the Smoke; the rising of the Sun from the west; the manifestation of the Beast; the Holy Qur'an will be taken up into heaven, and the Fire which will drive the people to their final gathering place. When the first of these major signs appear, the others will come soon after in quick succession. There is however, no definitive authority on the exact sequence in which all these greater signs will appear. The lesser signs are of Man's making whereas the major signs will be Divinely inspired.

During the course of the rest of this Chapter we will briefly touch upon some of the major portents of the Final Hour.

THE DAJJAL

It should be noted that the word 'Dajjal' does not appear in the Holy Qur'an. It does however; appear in various Ahadith collections, including the two Sahih Collections, Al-Bukhari and Al-Muslim.

Certainly, we cannot literally accept the common metaphorical descriptions of the Dajjal. To do so would be an absurdity – a distortion of logic and rationality. A rational approach to the subject suggests that the Dajjal will be an enterprise exhibiting several facets operating on multiple level fields. First and foremost, the Dajjal will be an individual – a charismatic global political leader. In the Christian Apocalypse he is described as the Anti-Christ. The Dajjal will also represent a global cultural phenomenon having the power to manipulate all streams of media information. The Dajjal as an ideology will command economic supremacy. Ahmad Thomson, in his book *Dajjal*, has also explained the phenomenon of the Dajjal with three aspects. There is Dajjal the individual, Dajjal as a global social and cultural phenomenon and Dajjal as an unseen force.

As an individual the Dajjal will have global reach, with the power to draw the masses to his cause. He will be conceived from global economic chaos, socio-political upheaval and lack of moral values. Today the global economy is essentially based on unethical accumulation of capital based on Riba (interest) manipulated by financial institutions and vested stakeholders. Riba is forbidden in Islam. The very rich thrive while the middle and working classes find their financial circumstances constrained. With Europe and the United States slowly coming out of a deep recession, we are looking at interesting times ahead. History teaches us that economic chaos often produces despots who impose tyrannical rule.

A master liar and manipulator, his sight will be constrained to that of evil. To get an understanding of the Dajjal, he will embody the traits and circumstances of both Napoleon and Hitler but on an unprecedented scale. The Dajjal will seek global conquest and therefore, naturally be in command of a mighty military force. No place will remain unscathed except, according to numerous Ahadith, the holy cities of Mecca and Medina. Some will argue that the platform for the arrival of Dajjal, the individual is already under way.

ALLAH will test our faith through the portents of the Hour, including the tribulations of the Dajjal. One important fact is that the Dajjal will seek the destruction of the followers of the three Abrahamic Faiths, not just Islam, pitting one against the other.

THE MAHDI

The Mahdi (the 'guided one') will be no prophet but an exemplary and rightly-guided political leader. He will restore justice and fairness under Qur'anic guidance, overcoming injustice and oppression. Though the Mahdi is not specifically mentioned by name in the Holy Qur'an, in the Tirmidhi and Abu Dawud Hadith collections however, the Prophet Muhammad is recorded as describing the Madhi as a man from His household, i.e. a descendant of His daughter Fatimah. He will have the same name as the Prophet, while the Mahdi's father's name will be the same as the Prophet's father.

As recorded in the Hadith of Ahmad Ibn Hanbal and Ibn Majah, the Prophet states that ALLAH will inspire the Mahdi, preparing him to carry out his task successfully. Though his rule will be brief, only seven years, within that time nevertheless the Mahdi will confront the many tribulations of the Dajjal. The Mahdi will unify Muslims under one political-religious banner and that is 'One Ummah'. He will also face many battles including confrontations in Syria and the battle for the conquest of Palestine. In order to achieve fairness and justice in the world, just as Jesus had overturned the tables of the money changers at the Temple Mount, so too will the Mahdi strike out against a global economy based on greed, interest (riba) and economic disparity. Mismanagement of (natural) resources is the prime cause for much of the poverty in the developing world today.

In Shi'ite Islam, the Mahdi has become central to religious-political belief. The majority of Shi'ite Muslims believe that the Mahdi is Muhammad al-Mahdi, the Twelfth Imam, who was born in 869AD and was hidden by ALLAH at the age of five. He is still alive but has been in occultation, awaiting the time when ALLAH has decreed his return. Sunni Islam, however, believes that the Mahdi will be born into an ordinary Muslim family but will be Divinely inspired.

It comes as no surprise then that over the centuries various individuals have claimed to be the Mahdi. The notion of a Mahdi as a redeemer who will establish a universal social order based on justice overcoming oppression has lent itself to various interpretations leading to different claims by individuals during the course of Islamic history. They include Mirza Ghulam Ahmad, who founded the Ahmadiyya Movement. This movement has proved limited in scope and reach as mainstream Sunni Islam does not recognise Mirza Ghulam Ahmad as the true Mahdi. Followers of the Ahmadiyya Movement can be found in West Africa, the U.S. and Europe with sizeable adherents being of Pakistani decent.

THE SECOND COMING OF ISA (JESUS)

From a study of the Hadith collections of Al-Muslim, Ahmad Ibn Hanbal and ibn Majah, the second coming of Isa (Jesus), son of Mary, will occur after the appearance of the Dajjal (Antichrist) and the emergence of the Mahdi (the 'guided one'). Isa will descend in the midst of wars being fought between the armies of the Mahdi against the armies of the Dajjal. Isa's descent will be marked with Divine manifestations so that He may be recognised. He will then join the Mahdi forces in their wars against the Antichrist. Eventually, it will be Isa and not the Mahdi who will destroy the Antichrist in battle, following which everyone from the 'People of the Book' (Jews and Christians) will believe in Isa. In the Christian Apocalyptic narrative this final battle is referred to as the Battle of Armageddon. Isa will assume leadership of the worldwide community of Islam, since the Mahdi will have passed away by then. In Islamic Belief, Isa is considered to be a Prophet of Islam, He will therefore, uphold the teachings and laws of Islam. Consequently, there will be only one Ummah, i.e. the Community of Islam. It is narrated in numerous Ahadith that Isa will break the crosses (symbols of the crucifixion), outlaw the consumption of swine and abolish the Jizya tax.

This assumption of leadership by Isa is unlikely to be a smooth one, as the second coming of Isa, from an Islamic perspective, will absolutely undermine the institution of the Vatican and its vested stakeholders. Isa will set the record straight that He was neither the son of God nor crucified on the cross, confirming the Qur'anic narrative.

During Isa's rule peace and security will prevail on earth. There will begin a period of abundant wealth and prosperity. During Isa's time as well, the tribes of Ya'jooj and Ma'jooj (Gog and Magog) will manifest themselves, creating havoc on earth. By ALLAH's command these tribes will be destroyed. Isa's rule will be for around forty years, during which time He will marry. Upon His death Muslims will perform the Islamic funeral prayer for Him and then bury Him in the city of Medina in a grave that has been left vacant beside the Prophet Muhammad at the Masjid al-Nabawi alongside the rightly guided Caliphs Abu Bakr and Umar.

YA'JOOJ AND MA'JOOJ (GOG AND MAGOG)

At-Tabarani, on the authority of Abdullah ibn Amru, the Prophet Muhammad stated that Ya'jooj and Ma'jooj are descendants of Adam. Again Ibn Kathir on the authority of Abu Sai'd Al-Khudri reports that the Prophet mentioned that Ya'jooj and Ma'joog will represent two nations. From the Hadith collections of Tirmidhi it is apparent that they will be enormous in terms of numbers with multitudes of weapons dispersing themselves across the globe consuming the world's natural resources and creating havoc on earth. They will appear during the time of Isa (Jesus) after the destruction of the Dajjal. They are currently encased behind a barrier. (Whether that barrier is physical or metaphorical is a matter of conjecture). Isa, son of Mary will pray to ALLAH to dispel this evil. ALLAH will respond to the supplication of Isa by inflicting a plague among Ya'jooj and Ma'jooj that will destroy them. It is then that the Final Hour will be near at hand.

The end of days figures in the other two Abrahmic Faiths too. Judeo-Christian sources consist mainly of the Book of Daniel, Ezekiel, and the Book of Revelations, as well as some scattered sources within other books of the Old and New Testaments.

APPENDIX 1

The Prophets Mentioned in the Holy Qur'an

The Holy Qur'an mentions 25 of the most prominent Prophets by name. Of ALLAH's Prophets, four were sent with Books of Guidance. They are the Tawrat (Torah) revealed to Prophet Musa (Moses); the Zabur (Psalms) revealed to Prophet Dawud (David); the Injil (the original Gospel) revealed to Prophet Isa (Jesus) and the Qur'an revealed to the final Prophet and Messenger Muhammad. The first prophet was Adam and the last prophet is Muhammad (Peace Be Upon Them). Muslims believe the Prophets mentioned in the Holy Qur'an are all Prophets of Islam for they all preached the worship of and submission to the one true God.

Qur'anic name	Biblical name
Adam	Adam
Idris	Enoch
Nuh	Noah
Hud	–
Salih	Salih
Ibrahim	Abraham
Isma'il	Ishmael
Ishaq	Isaac
Lut	Lot
Ya'qub	Jacob
Yusuf	Joseph
Shu'aib	–
Ayyub	Job
Musa	Moses
Harun	Aaron
Dhu'l-Kifl	Ezekiel
Dawud	David
Sulaiman	Solomon
Ilias	Elias
Al Yasa	Elisha
Yunus	Jonah
Zakariyya	Zachariah
Yaha	John
Isa	Jesus
Muhammad	–

APPENDIX 2

Recommended Further Reading and Useful Websites

For readers requiring further in-depth analysis of the topics covered here the author strongly recommends the following books (or their subsequent editions) and websites. For some book titles the date quoted are of the reprints.

Quranic References

Abdel Haleem M.A.S., *The Qur'an* (OUP, 2010)

Al-Hilali Dr. M.T. & Khan Dr. M.M., *Interpretation of the Meanings of The Noble Qur'an* (Darussalam, 1999)

Pickthall M, *The Meaning of the Glorious Qur'an* (Taj, 1986)

Rodwell J.M., *The Koran* (Phoenix, 2009)

The Presidency of Islamic Researchers, IFTA, Call and Guidance, *The Holy Qur-an, English Translations of the Meanings and Commentary* (King Fahd Holy Qur'an Printing Complex, 1405 AH)

Hadith References

Khan Dr. M.M, *Summarized Sahih Al-Bukhari* (Darussalam, 1996)

Textbook References

Armstrong K, *The Battle For God* (HarperCollins, 2000)

Armstrong K, *Islam, A Short History* (Phoenix 2001)

Armstrong K, *Muhammad, A Biography of the Prophet* (Phoenix, 2004)

Aslan R, *No God But God* (Arrow Books, 2006)

Esack F, *The Qur'an, A User's Guide* (Oneworld, 2005)

Horrie C & Chippendale P, *What is Islam* (Virgin Books, 2003)

Kathir I, *The Signs Before The Day of Judgement* (Dar Al Taqwa, 2007)

Lewis B, *The Crisis of Islam* (Phoenix, 2004)

Lunde P, *Islam A Brief History* (DK, 2005)

Muhammad F.N., *Islamiat For Students* (Ferozsons, 2001)

Rogerson B, *The Prophet Muhammad, A Biography* (Abacus, 2004)

Ruthven M, *Islam, A Very Short Introduction* (OUP, 2000)

Sarwar G, *Islam, Beliefs And Teachings*
(The Muslim Education Trust, 1982)

Taylor A, *The rise and fall of Great Empires* (Quercus, 2008)

Thomson A, *Dajjal, The King who has no clothes* (Ta-Ha, 1995)

Wilkinson P, *Religions* (DK, 2008)

Websites

www.aljazeera.com
www.bbc.co.uk
www.guardian.co.uk
www.genocidewatch.com
www.independent.co.uk
www.ochaopt.org
www.pewforum.org
www.rt.com
www.reuters.com
www.telegraph.co.uk
www.un.org

About the Author

Sheikh Mohammed Jakir Ahmed Jabbar was born into a 'progressive' Muslim family in South Wales, United Kingdom. He owes much of his moral fibre to the teachings he received in his formative years as a primary school student attending St. Joseph's Convent and St. Mary's Catholic School in Newport, South Wales. During his time there he regularly attended Bible-reading sessions. This sense of moral awareness was reinforced when his parents moved back to Dhaka, Bangladesh and the author was introduced to the world of Islam by the Ulemas of the neighbouring Sobhanbagh Mosque. The author's sense of self-discipline was forged attending Scholastica tutorials and later Bhuiyan Academy in Dhaka. Deeply unsatisfied with the Ulemas' orthodox approach to the study of Islam, the author took it upon himself from his early teens to understand the core message of Islam by studying numerous English translations and interpretations of the Holy Qur'an and numerous Ahadith, as well as, works of Islamic scholars that were available at the time.

This intellectual thirst to understand the central message of Islam reinforced and consolidated itself well into his adulthood.

Returning to the United Kingdom to complete his undergraduate studies, the author graduated in law with honours from the University of Wolverhampton. A week after completing his final year examinations he lost the light of his life, his dear mother. His mother's premature death would have far-reaching consequences for his future that would set the direction of his life.

The author started his working career as a reporter for Hansard at the National Assembly for Wales. He subsequently served as Registrar and Archives Officer for the Legal Services Division at the Welsh Development Agency until April 2002. Taking a temporary break from his career in Wales, the author returned to Dhaka to take care of his late mother's business interests. During his time in Dhaka he also taught undergraduate students under the University of London LLB external curriculum at a private law academy and wrote a revision aid for students studying A-Level Government and Politics under EDEXCEL, which proved extremely successful. In 2004 the author founded Renascence Publications. Mr Jabbar later returned to Wales to pursue higher academic interests in 2005. He is presently studying for a Master's Degree in International Commercial Law with Northumbria University, Newcastle, under its Distance Learning Programme.

In addition to his present employment, the author had been actively involved in his Trade Union. In their annual elections, towards the end of 2011 the author was elected the PCS Wales Regional Committee Representative on the PCS National Black Members' Committee. Following on, in March 2013, the author was also elected the PCS South Wales Revenue and Customs

Branch BME Representative. Back in 2008 he served on the Steering Committee for the 'Spiritual Capital' Cardiff Project presenting the Muslim perspective. The author is an amateur poet and has had his poetry published in newspapers in Bangladesh and in numerous anthologies in the United Kingdom and the United States of America.

Following the death of his father in August 2010 the author was unanimously elected honorary co-chairperson of the Jamia Madania Kowmia Sheikh M. A. Jabbar Islamic Complex situated in Sreemongal, Sylhet, Bangladesh. This three-storey complex is a highly-acclaimed and widely-respected academic centre specializing in Islamic education and houses a mosque that can accommodate more than one thousand devotees during prayer times. The institution has had the privilege of being visited by acclaimed Islamic scholars from across the Indian subcontinent and the Middle East. Meanwhile, the Madrassah also imparts education in several disciplines to more than six hundred students. The author has been invited on numerous occasions to speak on 'Islamic tolerance and justice' at a number of annual Islamic conventions held in Sylhet that were attended by tens of thousands of devotees.

The author is an avid reader. His interests include the study of Islam, comparative religions, international trade and commercial law, post Cold War global politics, modern and contemporary European history and astronomy.